T0205182

"The Object Lessons
to magic: the books take ordinary—even banal—objects
and animate them with a rich history of invention,
political struggle, science, and popular mythology. Filled
with fascinating details and conveyed in sharp, accessible
prose, the books make the everyday world come to life.
Be warned: once you've read a few of these, you'll start
walking around your house, picking up random objects,
and musing aloud: 'I wonder what the story is behind
this thing?'"

Steven Johnson, author of *Where Good Ideas
Come From* and *How We Got to Now*

"In 1957 the French critic and semiotician Roland
Barthes published *Mythologies*, a groundbreaking
series of essays in which he analysed the popular
culture of his day, from laundry detergent to the face of
Greta Garbo, professional wrestling to the Citroën DS.
This series of short books, Object Lessons, continues
the tradition."

Melissa Harrison, *Financial Times*

"Though short, at roughly 25,000 words apiece, these
books are anything but slight."

Marina Benjamin, *New Statesman*

The joy of the series, of reading *Remote Control*, *Golf Ball*, *Driver's License*, *Drone*, *Silence*, *Glass*, *Refrigerator*, *Hotel*, and *Waste* (more titles are listed as forthcoming) in quick succession, lies in encountering the various turns through which each of their authors has been put by his or her object. As for Benjamin, so for the authors of the series, the object predominates, sits squarely center stage, directs the action. The object decides the genre, the chronology, and the limits of the study. Accordingly, the author has to take her cue from the *thing* she chose or that chose her. The result is a wonderfully uneven series of books, each one a *thing* unto itself."

Julian Yates, *Los Angeles Review of Books*

The Object Lessons project, edited by game theory legend Ian Bogost and cultural studies academic Christopher Schaberg, commissions short essays and small, beautiful books about everyday objects from shipping containers to toast. *The Atlantic* hosts a collection of 'mini object-lessons'. . . . More substantive is Bloomsbury's collection of small, gorgeously designed books that delve into their subjects in much more depth."

Cory Doctorow, *Boing Boing*

. . . a sensibility somewhere between Roland Barthes and Wes Anderson."

Simon Reynolds, author of *Retromania: Pop Culture's Addiction to Its Own Past*

OBJECT LESSONS

A book series about the hidden lives of ordinary things.

Series Editors:

Ian Bogost and Christopher Schaberg

Advisory Board:

Sara Ahmed, Jane Bennett, Jeffrey Jerome Cohen, Johanna Drucker, Raiford Guins, Graham Harman, renée hoogland, Pam Houston, Eileen Joy, Douglas Kahn, Daniel Miller, Esther Milne, Timothy Morton, Kathleen Stewart, Nigel Thrift, Rob Walker, Michele White.

In association with

BOOKS IN THE SERIES

traffic

PAUL JOSEPHSON

Bloomsbury Academic
An imprint of Bloomsbury Publishing Inc

B L O O M S B U R Y
NEW YORK • LONDON • OXFORD • NEW DELHI • SYDNEY

Bloomsbury Academic

An imprint of Bloomsbury Publishing Inc

1385 Broadway	50 Bedford Square
New York	London
NY 10018	WC1B 3DP
USA	UK

www.bloomsbury.com

**BLOOMSBURY and the Diana logo are trademarks of
Bloomsbury Publishing Plc**

First published 2017

© Paul Josephson, 2017

All rights reserved. No part of this publication may be reproduced or
transmitted in any form or by any means, electronic or mechanical, including
photocopying, recording, or any information storage or retrieval system,
without prior permission in writing from the publishers.

No responsibility for loss caused to any individual or organization acting
on or refraining from action as a result of the material in this publication
can be accepted by Bloomsbury or the author.

Library of Congress Cataloging-in-Publication Data
Names: Josephson, Paul R., author.
Title: Traffic / Paul Josephson.
Description: New York, NY, USA: Bloomsbury Academic, an imprint of
Bloomsbury Publishing Inc., 2017. | Series: Object lessons | Includes
bibliographical references and index.
Identifiers: LCCN 2016034474 (print) | LCCN 2016036054 (ebook) |
ISBN 9781501329333 (pbk.: alk. paper) | ISBN 9781501329340 (ePDF)
Subjects: LCSH: Traffic engineering–Popular works. | Traffic
calming–Popular works.
Classification: LCC HE333 .J67 2017 (print) | LCC HE333 (ebook) |
DDC 388.3/1–dc23
LC record available at https://lccn.loc.gov/2016034474

ISBN: PB: 978-1-5013-2933-3
ePub: 978-1-5013-2935-7
ePDF: 978-1-5013-2934-0

Series: Object Lessons

Cover design: Alice Marwick

Typeset by Deanta Global Publishing Services, Chennai, India
Printed and bound in the United States of America

CONTENTS

INTRODUCTION

Slow down! You move too fast!
You got to make the morning last!
Just kicking down the cobblestones.

—SIMON AND GARFUNKEL

The world's nations have spent trillions of dollars on traffic that permit more automobiles to enter our cities, strangling the life from them with congestion, spewing pollution, and destroying communities. Laboring under the mistaken belief that they can solve traffic by building wider, straighter, and better roads, they only encourage more traffic. Belatedly and grudgingly, some leaders and engineers have promoted traffic calming—for example speed bumps—to slow it, to keep it at home in favor of public transportation, and to transform our cities again into quieter, safer places for children, walking dogs, mothers, and fathers.

Traffic takes many forms: the weekend odyssey, the morning rush, evening gridlock, the snarl-up, logjam, roadblock, and congestion; the slow-down, blockage, hold-up, and always the stoppage. Istanbul, Moscow, and Beijing have ground to a halt. Americans spend more and more time stuck in their automobiles every year; some people spend several hours a day, and thus entire days every year, behind the wheels of a vehicle.

Traffic grew in fits and starts at the beginning of the twentieth century. Then, as Ford Model-Ts, Chevrolets, Duesenbergs, Fiats and Hudsons, Nashes, Olds, and Packards entered the streets it overwhelmed human spaces and human sentimentalities. City fathers, construction companies, and citizens' groups thought they could handle traffic simply by building more roads, always by building more roads. But the automobile clogged each new highway, inexorably taking over daily life, and bringing the blights of noise, pollution, accidents, and more traffic. The Sunday drive. The parkway. The service station. Motels and roadside restaurants. The automobile with heater and windshield. Parking garages. And traffic.

Traffic-calming measures are as yet only a cry in the mechanical wilderness. A series of simple and inexpensive measures—technologies, laws, modifications of driving behavior—can improve the situation. They include speed bumps, traffic circles (also called "roundabouts"), signage, and fines. They may be more expensive and complex: rebuilding roadways to narrow them, providing dedicated bikeways, and creating entire neighborhoods free from traffic, such as pedestrian malls and the *woonerf* (living yard) employed in the Netherlands.

The only hope may be to rage against the machine. There are more than one billion automobiles in the world. China, in second place behind the United States, has 240 million vehicles and 120 million passenger cars, and recently became the first country to sell 20 million vehicles in one year. Even Inner Mongolia has three million cars. The Chinese burn 2.5 million barrels of oil daily to feed their vehicles. More than 1,500 new automobiles enter gridlocked, pollution-choked Beijing every day. And 70,000 Chinese die annually in automobile accidents, giving rise to the urban myth that drivers intentionally hit pedestrians. Truly, Chinese drivers have earned the reputation as awful drivers—crazy, cranky, inexperienced, ignorant of the law, and inattentive.

How can Chinese, Dutch, Brazilian, Uruguayan, New Zealand, French, Mexican, Argentinean, American or Russian officials slow traffic where pedestrians abound and discourage traffic when drivers insist on clogging the roads? One way is the speed bump. The speed hump. The *verkeersdrempel* (the Netherlands). *Lombada* (Brazil) or *lomada* (small hill, Uruguay). Judder bar (New Zealand). *Gendarme-dos-d'âne-ralentisseur* (France). *Tope* (limit, Mexico), *lomo de burro* (the donkey's back, Argentina), or *tummulo* (the burial mound, El Salvador, Guatemala, Honduras). And everywhere—the sleeping policeman (*policies acostados* or лежачий полицейский in Russian).[1]

The speed bump is a hump, platform, or other rise affixed horizontally across the roadway, made of asphalt, concrete, or plastic, and intended to slow vehicular traffic while permitting fluid flow. Like signs and traffic signals, the speed bump is a simple technology that can be employed fearlessly to bring some order to a world of powerful machines and reestablish an appropriate hierarchy between pedestrians and automobiles. Introduced in the 1960s, the speed bump has become a popular means of traffic calming because of its low cost, simplicity, and effectiveness.

In China there are virtually no speed bumps, no roundabouts, and no driver pays attention to zebra crossings (painted pedestrian crosswalks). They seem to abide by the Beatles' philosophy, "You say yes, I say no. You say stop, and I say go, go, go." Yet you can buy speed bumps on the cheap from Alibaba, China's—and the world's—biggest online commercial site.[2] Slow down! You move too fast!

The speed bump cannot stand alone; it must be used with other traffic-calming measures—roundabouts, signs, signals, fines and tickets, rumble strips, street closures, pedestrian zones, and one-way streets. Otherwise, drivers seek other routes to avoid the bumps, and they create dangerous volumes and bottlenecks in other neighborhoods. The notion of "traffic calming," or *Verkehrsberuhigung* in the German language where it was introduced, dates to the 1980s. It seeks to slow traffic without generating more congestion and achieve greater safety for pedestrians, cyclists, and drivers and passengers. Although I drive, I'm all about *Verkehrsberuhigung*, and I walk or bicycle to work, and I'd like to live in a *woonerf*, the Dutch approach to *Verkehrsberuhigung*, that turns entire neighborhoods into pedestrian areas while forcing the car to sit quietly.

Traffic calming has class and race. Wealthier communities are more likely to have the resources and the will to install traffic-calming technologies. Those communities tend to be white and middle class, or university towns. An exception is Washington, DC, which is over 50 percent African American, yet has a simple online procedure to pursue traffic-calming measures.[3] DC has terrible traffic problems—it holds a firm position in America's top ten for traffic jams. Clearly, DC residents want to slow traffic to punish Congress for failing to give them full representation. They cannot elect to Congress. So they vote with speed bumps so that congresspeople will have to sit in traffic to think about their refusal to vote on the National Highway Trust Fund.

The speed bump and other traffic technologies have gender. Or at least, auto safety has gender because the crash test dummies on which engineers experiment to improve the "crashworthiness" of vehicles and make roads safer until quite recently were essentially "male" in their weight, size, and shape characteristics. Speed bumps, crashworthiness, and *Verkehrsberuhigung* should be for all citizens of the world, black and white, male and female, transgendered, poor and wealthy.

Traffic calming has both physicality and symbolic value. It suggests that citizens, pedestrians, parents with strollers, environmentalists, and policy makers in fact have tools at their disposal to fight the seemingly omniscient and heretofore unchallenged power of the automobile. In a slower, safer world traffic calming is the happy resolution of conflicts between mayors, traffic planners, automobile owners, neighborhood leaders, bicyclists, and traditional and modern families who have managed to create a safer and quieter place to walk.

My first intellectual encounter with a speed bump was along the Trans-Amazonian Highway. The intellectual cacophony of nature (the Amazonian rainforest), modernity (a highway intended to promote settlement and rapid economic development), and a neo-Luddite tool for traffic calming (under 0.5 inhabitants per square kilometer) slowed me down, bumped my thoughts, and led me to curved roads, dedicated bicycle lanes, greenways, and traffic calming.

Fighting the speed bump at every turn of the wheel is automobility. Automobility is automobiles, trucks, motorcycles, and mopeds; concrete, asphalt, dirt, and gravel roads; signs, signals, guardrails, and medians; the petrochemical industry, oil and gas corporations, drilling enterprises, and gas stations; tankers and pipelines; and especially the automotive industry. It is citizens who embrace the automobile for its seeming freedom of motion and convenience, but receive mass-produced individuality. It is public transportation that has fallen apart because of the power of the automobile to grow its own infrastructure omnisciently, and because of the manufacturers' seeming ability to dictate the abandonment of mass transit and even of sidewalks. While many societies support extensive public transportation systems, most American towns have given up on them. Congress has destroyed the passenger train because it hates subsidies for transport, but gives generous ones to oil.

Finally, automobility is a built environment that enables the automobile to move about while pushing other human activities—walking and strolling, resting and playing, and working and living in spaces with inadequate greenery, ventilation, and quiet—to the side. Automobility is straight roads; houses, buildings, and stores oriented to maximize space devoted to thoroughfares and parking lots; the public health and environmental costs of pollution and accidents; and barrels of money spent on infrastructure, repairs, and distant wars to ensure the flow of oil. Only speed bumps offer solace as the pea in the automobile's bed.

Initially, seeing the automobile as salvation, crucial to commerce, and the epitome of progress, policy makers and engineers joyously did all they could to spread its reach and increase its speed. They pushed pedestrians aside, ignored parks, removed houses and apartments for roads and parking spaces. These same individuals belatedly recognized the extensive environmental and public health costs of automobility, but only recently have taken steps to calm machines and emphasize human aesthetics.

In this book I refer to a variety of traffic-calming measures with a focus on the speed bump. I mean speed bumps both narrowly—the speed bump itself—and symbolically, as a metaphor for what can be accomplished simply and cheaply to improve the quality of life wherever automobility threatens it. The speed bump thus includes both the thing in itself and the things that make it—people, automobiles, roads, companies, scientists, researchers. It includes entire neighborhoods calmed from automobile assault (the *woonerf* and the pedestrian mall, for example), other simple calming devices (the roundabout), and safer roads and vehicles ("crashworthiness"). From the appearance of the first vehicles to mass production, from the growing involvement of governments in building roads, to the expense of ever greater shares of local, state, and national budgets on automobility, from the beliefs of presidents, queens, tycoons, and citizens that automobiles are a symbol of national vitality, to the growing worry among engineers, lawyers, and officials about accidents, death, and injury, we will take a bumpy journey from the dawn of the automobile to the speed bump and to contemporary efforts at traffic calming in the United States, Northern Europe, Brazil, and Russia.

What has slowed the spread of speed bumps and other calming technologies? Though often aware of the possibility that one calming measure might divert traffic onto another street, city planners focused on "spot improvements" one block or street at a time because they found it too difficult to reach

FIGURE 1 Speedbump and Pedestrian Crossing, in Severodvinsk, Russia, a nuclear shipbuilding city on the White Sea, July 2016.
Courtesy of KatherineGo.

agreement with individuals and groups across neighborhoods, and because comprehensive calming plans were much more costly than a ribbon of tar or two. The jurisdictions have had to rely on local and state, not federal, funding, which limits their ability—and resources—to embrace comprehensive plans,[4] while bitter disputes among neighbors and the opposition of emergency, fire, and police officials have created their own bumps in the way of speed bumps.[5] For example, in 2013 a Queen Street, Newtown, Connecticut, resident pushed the local police commission to finish installing all five speed bumps planned for a main street in a battle against the vocal opposition of rabid speeding motorists. Another group fought to remove all speed bumps on Queen Street because they saw it as the gateway to the commercial center of Newtown, served emergency services, and was not a "private road as much as a few people would like it to be." Rather, speed bumps were an "eyesore" and "waste of money."[6]

1 MUSHROOMS IN MINSK

Like police, speed bumps occupy a visible presence in the authoritarian regime of Aleksander Lukashenka in Belarus. They grow like mushrooms in Minsk. In the middle of 2012 there were nearly 800 "sleeping policemen" in Minsk, a 250 percent increase since 2005, and a total of 6,000 in the country, some curved, others trapezoidal. Designers have gotten more sophisticated about placement and geometry. They chose designs taking into account the longitudinal and transverse slope, the roadway profile, the need for drainage, and the impact of snow and ice and their removal. They placed them within 20–30 meters of places of frequent accident sites or other dangerous stretches of the road, and within 5–10 meters of or directly at pedestrian crossings, especially near parks, stadiums, public transit, schools, and shops.[1] Many municipalities opt for plastic speed bumps because of ease of installation, variety of shapes, fewer problems with drainage, and visibility because of inset reflectors. They can easily be removed before winter to facilitate snow plowing. They cost

3,000 rubles ($50) per meter of length.[2] There are also real sleeping policemen, those who fall asleep on the job, and risk being fired.[3]

Omnipotent motorists universally complain about traffic calming, declaring that speed bumps decay into rubble, appear too frequently out of the fog of pedestrian movement, and old warning markings have rubbed off, all of which threaten the suspensions of their cars. And then there's the practice of parking hither and thither, helter and skelter, wherever they stop. But the Minsk traffic engineers will not back off, and promise to add traffic islands and barriers to sleeping policeman to engage the automobile in battle. The Minskian engineers tried small roundabouts, too, and faced an angry backlash from citizens too cowed to face down the authoritarian regime in other matters. Engineers have determined that safe intersections require more "mini-traffic rings." And there will be more bedridden sleeping policemen.[4]

Public transportation offers another solution to traffic. With its population approaching 2 million people, Minsk has determined to build sixteen new metro stations, tack on one long addition to one subway line by 2020, and has begun using eminent domain to remove people from some neighborhoods for a new, fourth line (in theory by 2030) with seventeen beautiful new well-illuminated modern stations to supplement the existing thirty-five stations.[5]

Some people strangely disparage speed bumps for inordinate cost. Yet speed bumps are cheap at $1,500–$4,000 depending on size and function, and certainly faster to install than a new metro line. One sleeping policeman costs a granule of US federal spending for transportation that in 2014 alone was $165 billion for highways, $65 billion for mass transit, and $36 billion for aviation. Since 1956 transportation spending has averaged between 2.5 and 3.0 percent of GDP.[6] Imagine the costs of *not* installing speed bumps. Discouraging traffic means no need to expand infrastructure for automobiles. Narrowing roads for sidewalks and bike paths means fewer repairs. Traffic calming leads to segregation of traffic from other human activities, and also lower emissions, noise, and dangers so that public health improves.[7]

Traffic calming works. Through its determined pursuit of calming measures, Sweden has achieved one of the world's lowest automobile fatality rates, and at 6.67/100,000 inhabitants, the lowest in the EU, with a goal to lower fatalities to zero. The Swedes had great success to some degree, although there are still some 400–500 deaths annually. It achieved this through safer roads, emphasis on road-user responsibilities, safer conditions for cyclists, compulsory use of winter tires, better road traffic designs, better handling of traffic offenses, involvement of voluntary organizations, and calming.[8] Everywhere the installation of humps, bumps, and roundabouts reduced speeds and numbers of accidents, and often traffic volumes near the devices decline.[9]

Why speed bumps and dedicated bicycle lanes? Promotion of cycling and walking as an alternative to short urban car trips is not enough. Pedestrians and cyclists face significant risks as road users. Slowing automobiles and providing dedicated pathways contributes to a decrease in the absolute number of cyclist fatalities. In the Netherlands the number of fatalities among cyclists was 54 percent lower in 1998 as compared to 1980, in spite of the increase in both car use and bicycle use. In Germany the total number of cyclist fatalities fell by 66 percent between 1975 and 1998, while the share of cycling in transport increased substantially from about 8 percent to 12 percent of all trips. In York, UK, the number of cyclists killed or seriously injured was halved from 1991 to 1998 at the same time as the cycling level rose.[10]

When speed bumps entered the pantheon of traffic-calming measures engineers worried more about legal and safety obstacles to their use more than welcomed them. If drivers passed over them too quickly and damaged their cars' suspensions, would they sue? Such questions postponed their wide use until the 1980s. Early studies on design geometries (heights, placement, and shapes) were not hopeful for arriving at the universal bump that posed no threat to the vehicle. Researchers, thinking more about the inconvenience to the car than the safety of pedestrians, concluded that speed bumps were not entirely effective at reducing vehicle speeds; were an immediate hazard to some vehicles (bicycles, motorcycles, and so on); that it was impossible to design an effective, narrow speed bump for all types of vehicles; and that speed bumps would cause noise pollution in residential neighborhoods.[11] But the whole point was to inconvenience the automobile, not to worry about its feelings.

A Dutch study conducted for the Swedish government in 2003 sought to combine engineering and social principles in designs. Traffic calming was "a combination of network planning and engineering measures to enhance road safety as well as other aspects of livability for the citizens." Its goal was to discourage motorized through-traffic, slow the remaining traffic, and support walking and cycling. In residential and shopping areas this was easier than for thoroughfares. The researchers admitted that local residents were so often dismayed by traffic calming that it had to be accompanied by "public participation, information and education" that communicated the positive effects of traffic calming to them.[12]

How bumpy has the road to traffic-calming measures been? What explains their grudging acceptance? What of the epistemology of *Verkehrsberuhigung*? A bit of urbane philosophy and urban history will help to explore these questions.

2 SPEED BUMPS IN TWENTIETH-CENTURY PHILOSOPHY

Bertrand Russell, Ludwig Wittgenstein, Jacques Derrida, Hannah Arendt, and the Vienna School philosophers share the fact that they wrote nothing about speed bumps. I, a neo-materialist, am surprisingly weak in the area of the philosophy of asphalt. Thankfully, Bruno Latour has written about speed bumps, especially as a social constructionist, although now he is recognized for his work in actor-network theory that treats objects as part of social networks. He maintains that a dualism between human and nonhuman things makes no sense. Humans have given a kind of agency to the traffic-calming objects; the speed bump is an object—a nonhuman!—that participates in the systems of our lives.

Speed bumps, when used in conjunction with signs, signals, and other objects, slow automobile drivers in most instances. They force people to yield, give priority to pedestrians and cyclists. Speed bumps "understand" that the automobile's own seeming autonomy must be seen as a social force and yield to other social forces. Latour argues that in this way the speed bump has a range of social roles. It is not merely asphalt, plastic, or concrete, but serves a moral function by requiring people to behave in ways that we believe they ought to. He thus rejects the view that speed bumps and other technologies are passive tools and the view the objects are some kind of self-augmenting and autonomous technology.

Police have many responsibilities to interdict crime, offer citations, protect the safety and welfare of the public, and so on. To many people, they are over-armed, trained for interdiction of criminals, and have little time for traffic safety; in fact, police are relatively rarely involved in directing traffic or in pulling drivers over, except in corrupt societies where they use traffic stops to shake down bribes. In some cases police periodically station themselves in particularly dangerous areas where they can hide, or because of heavy traffic, and use radar to catch speeders. In many communities, police serve as revenue generators. In infamous Ferguson, Missouri, a St. Louis suburb of about 21,000 residents, where the unarmed Michael Brown was shot at twelve times by a policeman, the local government took in more than $2.5 million in municipal court revenue in a recent fiscal year, largely by stopping citizens for minor infractions of the law—disproportionately people of color—in order to balance its budget. A number of communities in St. Louis County rely on fines for between 10 and 40 percent of their revenue.[1] Ferguson police were illegal speed bumps, and the US Department of Justice intervened.

If police are doing other things, then speed bumps have taken on the function of the policeman. In authoritarian regimes, words and laws are not enough to moderate behavior, and hardly guarantee the rule of law. In Russia, real policemen, in particular the notorious GAIchniki, now called "police," engage in arbitrary enforcement of laws, shakedowns, and constant "checking of documents" in pursuit of bribes. I have silently witnessed this from inside an automobile in Russia as a few hundred rubles ended a pullover. Police also sleep on the job. And the state has turned to sleeping policemen, especially in the more affluent European cities, while less so in the Urals region and Siberia.

Yet, as Latour points out, even if the message to slow down is the same whether by policeman or by speed bump, the meaning differs depending on whether the driver enters into communication with the police officer or with the "materiality" of the speed bump. A police officer uses hand signals, batons, whistles, sirens, and radar guns to slow the driver, while the speed bump uses its shape and size to slow driver who will otherwise risk damage to the vehicle and his/her own discomfort. Cities use signs to ensure compliance with speed and other laws, but they do not work the way that speed bumps do with their materiality. Latour observes that speed bumps reveal the legal, organizational, and social forces behind technologies, the engineers, traffic planners, road crews, and their associated institutions of urban planning and maintenance. Latour writes, "The speed bump is ultimately not made of matter; it is full of engineers and chancellors and lawmakers, commingling their wills and their story lines with those of gravel, concrete, paint, and standard calculations."[2] In a word, objects are hardly objects alone, but are objects intermediated in and by society. Human labor is required for objects, and those objects exist being their "materiality." But enough of theory of speed bumps. What of utopian visions of speed bumps?

3 UTOPIAN VISIONS OF MACHINES AND PEOPLE: A WORLD WITHOUT SPEED BUMPS

Architectural visionaries of the 1920s and 1930s incorporated automobiles in their designs, with some of those designs including traffic. For the most part, however, the inclusion of automobility meant the diminution of human aesthetics. Most futurists envisaged the world as a giant factory and huge skyscrapers, not of soot-shooting smokestacks, clanging machines, and teeming streets, but of domesticated technology of broad thoroughfares without horses and heavy vehicles, of clean, efficient, and harmonious nature operating quietly according to man's will.[1]

Radburn, a community in Bergen County, New Jersey, in 1929 was a town for the "motor age." Its planners, Clarence

Stein, Henry Wright, and Marjorie Sewell, followed the garden city movement of Ebenezer Howard that arose in the 1890s with cities as planned communities surrounded by "greenbelts" and with balanced areas of residences, industry, and agriculture. Howard's idea in *Garden Cities of Tomorrow* (1902) was to have relatively economically dependent cities, with sunlight and cleanliness, not the din of industry, and with short commutes and the preservation of the countryside. Transportation times and costs would be kept down by small and efficient connections between work and production. Howard predicted in 1913 that the bicycle was sufficient for transport of the laborer to make his way to work.[2]

Stein, Wright, Mumford, and others who founded the Regional Planning Association of America (RPAA) in 1923 planned to separate traffic with a pedestrian path system that did not cross any major roads, and with such innovations as "culs-de-sac" that not only discouraged but also precluded drive-through traffic.[3] They hoped to reform US urban planning practices with a focus on high-density urban housing that preserved green landscape through central courtyards, with peripheral roads and these culs-de-sac; little could they understand how a laissez-faire attitude to the automobile destroyed utopian plans for green, quiet cities.

During the New Deal, President Franklin Roosevelt supported a greenbelt town program for city building, not necessarily to create better urban communities, but to expand jobs and provide affordable housing for low-income workers during the Great Depression. The Resettlement

Administration responsible for the program employed Stein, who presented guidelines that included community-based ideas with environmental and noise standards for three greenbelt towns: Greenbelt, Maryland; Greenhills (outside of Cincinnati), Ohio; and Greendale (outside of Milwaukee), Wisconsin.[4] Stein pushed his postwar town-planning program to include pedestrian-friendly designs for neighborhoods and towns in his *Toward New Towns for America* (1951).

The automobile also figured in Frank Lloyd Wright's utopian Broadacre City in his *The Disappearing City* (1932). Wright described a community of 1-acre plots of land and houses on them whose activities, including democratic governance, were facilitated by the automobile. As others have noted, Wright was a strict individualist and he believed Americans must be "liberated from the domination of an acquisitive, inhumanly standardized economic order." Each family in Broadacre City would have its own inexpensive house, with farmers living on 10-acre lots near community centers, with smaller, well-ventilated and illuminated factories, design centers, schools, and so on.[5] Pedestrian safety existed within the 1-acre plots, not beyond them. Indeed, Broadacre City celebrated burgeoning suburbs fully dependent on the automobile.

Yet the automobile was the problem, not the solution. As Howard Strong wrote in 1927, "Modern development of rapid transit, of means of communication, and the almost universal use of the automobile" melded cities and suburbs into an economic and social unit. That interrelationship had "immensely complicated the traffic problem of the metropolitan area. There is endless going to and fro, from somewhere to somewhere else—the worker is separated from his employer, the buyer from the seller, the producer from the distributor and the consumer, the amuser from the amused—a multiplicity of contacts has arisen-all producing traffic on the streets and highways, and bringing highway engineers, police departments and the traveling public well-nigh to desperation."[6]

Colin Buchanan's *Traffic in Towns* (1963) may have opened the modern traffic-calming movement. Perhaps the first such government report, it did not make specific policy recommendations, but in an academic tone considered traffic problems, causes, effects, and solutions. The report was healthy in its democracy by keeping in mind the citizen who lived in towns increasingly overwhelmed by automobiles, who may own a car, and who voted. The report addressed "the possibilities of adapting towns to motor traffic before there is any question of applying restrictive measures."[7] It documented the growing concentration and at times paralysis of traffic. The side effects—accidents, noise, fumes, intrusion into daily life, and degradation of the environment—were there to stay.[8] The report seemed to recommend such traffic calming on main roads, with local neighborhoods protected by one-way streets and closures to prevent through traffic. In theory, traffic and roads would be subservient to the environmental requirements for living and working. In practice, this was a volume control approach, not speed control measures, and it was another two decades before Britain systematically applied any such measures.

Almost forty years ago a Virginia traffic engineer observed the obvious: wide, flat streets with broad curves and good sight distances encouraged speed and attracted through traffic, while narrow streets with "poor geometrics" had the opposite effects. When the roads and intersections filled, commuters often sought faster routes through adjacent residential areas. They might not save distance, but they saved time, and they also brought noise, pollution, and risk to pedestrians in those neighborhoods. In the 1970s as a first step to deal with these growing traffic problems planners focused on signs and signals. Four-way stop signs were very popular, but were ineffective in reducing speed, and drivers often rolled through them. Yield signs hardly had an impact. Speed limit signs that dropped legal speeds to 25 mph had potential, but the percentage of individuals speeding increases generally the lower the speed limit. On the other hand, "No Trucks," "One-Way," and "Do Not Enter" signs seemed to reduce maximum hourly volume. Signals were used as a last resort because of their high cost and the fact they did not fit in every neighborhood. Planners therefore learned a second approach, "geometry": diverters, "T" intersections, traffic circles, narrowing street width, landscaped medial strips, culs-de-sac and barricades, and street closures, the last three quite unpopular.[9] Bumps and humps were modern geometry, yet so simple and inexpensive.

Growing evidence of the immediate utility of traffic calming soon presented itself. In *Livable Streets* (1981) Donald Appleyard contended that residents on streets with light traffic had more friends and twice as many acquaintances as those who lived on streets with heavy traffic.[10] Appleyard, who pursued community-based planning for neighborhoods based on recognition of the negative impact of automobiles on people's lives and personal feelings and psychologies, and who researched the "effects of traffic upon the lives of local residents, the physical characteristics of cities as fulfilling and joyful places to live, how to manage traffic in residential

FIGURE 2 Traffic in Detroit, ca. 1915. Automobiles had already clogged streets early in the century.
Detroit Publishing Company Photograph Collection, Library of Congress, Washington, DC, LC-DIG-det-4a27913.

areas, conservation of neighborhoods and the like," died "an innocent victim of a senseless, speeding automobile. . . ."[11]

Most observers acknowledge that Carmen Hass-Klau first introduced the notion of *Verkehrsberuhigung*, and first wrote about it in English in 1985, although several city planners had sought some armistice with the automobile since the 1920s. The car was victorious at nearly every juncture, using the armistices to claim more land, lay more asphalt, pour more

FIGURE 3 Delivery Trucks Jamming West 37th Street.
Al Aumuller, New York World and Telegram Photo, 1945, Library of Congress, Washington, DC, ID cph 3c11255, Reproduction number LC-USZ62-111255.

concrete, and force the redesign of more and more cities and suburbs. In *The Pedestrian and City Traffic* (1990), Hass-Klau gave a one-hundred-year history of the destruction of cities by motor traffic and the failure of (German) traffic planners to save their cities from the automobile.[12] In *Civilized Streets* (1992), a history of *Verkehrsberuhigung*, Hass-Klau and his co-authors went further in a comparative work to assimilate information and experience on traffic calming in England, Netherlands, Germany, Denmark, and Sweden.[13]

4 MUMFORD AND MOSES

These ideas played out in a battle for the soul of the city among city planners and architects. The automobile would win. Lewis Mumford, an insightful analyst of the place of technology in society, trained as an architect, persistently criticized the design of cities, or rather the way in which they had evolved—helter-skelter—as enablers of machines, blotters of the sun, and usurpers of green spaces. In the 1930s Mumford seemed to support the plans of Robert Moses, the all-powerful head of the Port Authority, to expand massively the network of New York metropolitan area bridges, roads, tunnels, and highways to solve growing traffic problems. But by the 1940s Mumford recognized that Moses saw only highways, never the problems they caused, and he found Moses's highways purposely placed in poor city neighborhoods with especially desperate prospects for the powerless. Moses turned Riverside Park along the Hudson River into a highway, too. Mumford carried out his struggle for a city of people, not automobiles and towering skyscrapers, and his battle with Moses, in a monthly column, "Skyline," in the *New Yorker*, a number of whose essays were republished in book form.[1]

Already in the 1920s Mumford worried about the fact that one-third of city residents lived without decent housing and in poor work conditions. Their long, monotonous daily commutes, the thick fumes and suffocating din of the workplaces, the absence of any view or variety or green or sunlight, a city more and more divorced from the out-of-doors, the overcrowding of the parks—all of these things exhausted them and deprived them of health and happiness, and many had resulted from the imperative of the automobile. The wealthy lived well but apart from the poor, while the city streets were "vastly overtaxed by the traffic of their automobiles." Mumford believed in new roads as solutions to the problems of clogged avenues, crime, and congestion. Unfortunately, the city continued to grow, and in "its blind and heedless growth" had wiped out its natural environment.[2]

Eventually Mumford saw that automobiles were the problem, and he sought calming measures to turn the city into a place to live, not a "shambles" and a magnet for them. Building roads was not the way. Mumford wrote, "Like the tailor's remedy for obesity—letting out the seams of the trousers and loosening the belt—this does nothing to curb the greedy appetites that have caused the fat to accumulate." He presciently continued,

"Future generations will perhaps wonder at our willingness, indeed our eagerness, to sacrifice the education of our children, the care of the ill and aged, the development of the arts, to say nothing of ready access to nature, for the lopsided system of mono-transportation, going through low density areas at sixty miles an hour, but reduced in high density areas to a bare six. But our descendants will perhaps understand . . . if they realize that our cities are being destroyed for the same superstitious religious ritual: the worship of speed and empty space. Lacking sufficient municipal budgets to deal adequately with all of life's requirements that can be concentrated in the city, we have settled for a single function, transportation, or rather for a single part of an adequate transportation system, locomotion by private motor car. . . ."[3]

He railed against the automobile as a "sacred cow of the American religion of technology," for which no public expenditure appeared too great.

Mumford did not reject technology like a Luddite. He knew technological systems could be designed with a human aesthetics rather than military- or business-oriented aesthetic. He pursued what he called *neotechnics* that were built on recognition of interdependence of technologies with humans and environment. He saw electricity and automobiles as facilitating decentralization of population beyond the urban centers to satellite garden cities that preserved greenbelts. He sought boundaries for existing cities, not their interminable growth, that would ensure cities of human scale.[4] The pedestrian mall, the speed bump, the garden and park were but simple ways through technological choice to limit the cacophony of the machine age and to achieve human scales.

Rejecting Mumford's circumspection about the automobile, Robert Moses used his position as Port Authority chief to rebuild New York City for the middle class automobilist. He took advantage first of all of New Deal programs intended to put people back to work to fund a series of public works projects. His marvels of engineering—the Triborough, Henry Hudson, Throgs Neck, Bronx-Whitestone, and the Verrazano–Narrows bridges, and the Brooklyn-Queens and the Cross Bronx expressways—are now overburdened with traffic at all hours on all days and constantly under repair.

Moses seized on the opportunity of postwar prosperity—and a growing tax base, rapidly increasing automobile ownership, and urbanization—to accelerate public works projects in the name of urban renewal. He was "oblivious" to negative environmental impacts even as he pursued projects connected with the burgeoning interstate highway system. His roads drew concrete lines across the neighborhoods of people of color that forced them to move or to live proximate to exhaust, noise, and vistas of expressways; once these expressways were built, planners had no choice but to affix new ones to them, thus extending the unequal impact of highways on African Americans. Moses purposely designed parkway underpasses with a low arch to prevent public buses from being able to use them, his thinking being that fewer black people could afford automobiles and the majority of them would thus be prohibited from using his parkways to get to beaches on Long Island or parks upstate. He responded to accusations of racism with a wounded, lengthy open letter.[5]

Wherever he went, Moses befriended the automobile. He consulted with traffic planners in Portland, Oregon, on their growing traffic problems, and recommended roads, bridges, and parking garages, seeing the city essentially as a magnet for the automobile and the economic miracles it brought.[6] He believed that commerce, jobs, and culture would adhere to city centers, and did not anticipate how automobiles in fact fractured cities, had huge public health costs, and led to suburban development and white flight, not to the city's rejuvenation.

5 THE HISTORICAL CONCATENATION OF CONGESTION

As more people take to the road in automobiles, most as single occupants, the more roads become clogged with impatient drivers. Building new roads or widening existing thoroughfares only temporarily alleviates the situation; soon more cars join the fray. This is the "If you build it, they will come" conundrum of traffic. The only solution is to discourage automobile traffic through incentives and disincentives—taxes, fees, better public transport, safe bicycle lanes, and traffic-calming measures like speed bumps. Only the courageous have taken on the vehicle; in 1998 the mayor of Bogotá, Colombia, Enrique Peñalosa, said "no," fought off private bus mafias, created a massive public transit system, established one-fare to enable low-income riders, insisted on service to all neighborhoods, supported bicycle lanes, started car-free Sundays, and raised parking fees, in a short time defeating gridlock.[1]

American citizens and officials dreaded saying "no" to the automobile. Since the 1890s the US government has seen as its responsibility the spending of tax revenues to enable more vehicles to clog cities and to penetrate forests and national parks, in part as pushed by the transportation industry, logging operations, and other businesses. By the twenty-first century the US road network was the world's longest at about 6.6 million kilometers in total length, with roughly 4.3 million kilometers of paved roads including 76,334 kilometers of expressways.[2] As for bike paths? We really don't know, but perhaps there are ten major car-free bike paths in the entire nation.[3] In Germany, the bikeway network more than doubled in length, from 12,911 kilometers (8,070 mi) in 1976 to 31,236 kilometers (19,522 mi) in 1996. In the Netherlands, the bikeway network doubled in length, from 9,282 kilometers (5,801 mi) in 1978 to 18,948 kilometers (11,843 mi) in 1996.[4] Germany, with a population of 80 million people (one-quarter that of the United States), has bike lanes at one-third the length of the entire US interstate highway system. While the European countries pursued dedicated bike lanes, the United States unhaltingly embraced automobility and its imperative—traffic.

The Federal Highway Administration (FHWA) and its predecessors have engaged in an orgy of road construction for over one hundred years.[5] The Federal Aid Road Act of 1916 "established the basis for the Federal Aid highway program in cooperation with the states" to build and maintain rural post roads, from 1919 as the Bureau of Public Roads. As automobile ownership and traffic increased dramatically in the 1920s, so too did federal involvement in highway financing and construction, including for "parkways," parks for automobiles—for example, the Bronx River Parkway in Westchester County, New York, completed in the early 1920s and the first US road with a safety median strip, and the Mount Vernon Memorial Parkway, in the nation's capital, now part of the scenic George Washington Memorial Parkway, the site of the nation's most scenic traffic jams.[6]

Engineers and planners largely shared the belief that the road belonged to the automobile, not the pedestrian, and by extension that the city served the automobile. They worked to criminalize jaywalking in the 1920s and 1930s when people, horses, trade, and automobiles all tried to occupy the street; automobilists needed the street clean of these newly lawless human and animal obstacles to increase speed of motion.[7] The automobiles took over, people and animals left, speeds increased, businesses left downtown areas, commerce suffered, stores shuttered by 6:00 p.m., and cities lost their souls.

The automobile could not be slowed even in the Great Depression. Roads were crucial to the New Deal effort to put Americans back to work: road construction created jobs. The national park system expanded, as did the roads in them, for example in the Great Smoky Mountains National Park, the Shenandoah National Park, and the Everglades National Park. Construction on the Blue Ridge Parkway and Skyline Drive commenced in 1935 linking Shenandoah and Great Smoky Mountain National Parks. Seeing these roads only in a positive light, Bureau of Public Roads Division of Information head, Herbert Fairbank, published *Toll Roads and Free Roads* (1939), what has been called "the first formal description of what became the interstate highway system to support road construction as crucial to the future of cities and their commerce with goods and services moving without interruption by traffic jams."[8]

If during the Second World War construction in parks was suspended, then it accelerated postwar when it was seen

FIGURE 4 President Eisenhower signs the Federal-Aid Highway Act of 1954 on May 6, 1954, surrounded by senators and congressmans. Traffic has gender.
Courtesy Dwight Eisenhower Library, in collection of Federal Highway Administration, Department of Transportation, Washington, DC as accessed July 16, 2016, at http://www.fhwa.dot.gov/highwayhistory/resultsDisplayImg.cfm?img=il_19_aasho_54_17.jpg.

FIGURE 5 Interstate Route 10, the Santa Monica Freeway,
meets the Harbor Freeway in Los Angeles.
Courtesy of Federal Highway Administration, Department of
Transportation, Washington, DC as accessed July 16, 2016, at
http://www.fhwa.dot.gov/highwayhistory/resultsDisplayImg.
cfm?callPage=gallery.cfm&img=ca_1_I10_FHWA_63_1239.jpg&results=.

as central to economic growth, and as millions of Americans
bought vehicles. Symbolically, the US government moved
the Bureau of Public Roads to the Department of Commerce.
The passage of the Federal Aid Highway Act of 1956 to build
the National System of Interstate and Defense Highways, by
2013 at 48,000 miles (77,000 kilometers) and a cost of $450

billion, celebrated the joining of government, modern roads, and sleek fast automobiles and diesel digesting tractor-trailer rigs. The number of automobiles grew in the 1950s from 25 million to 70 million—and in 2015 to an unmanageable almost 260 million registered vehicles. In New York City in 2015 a *parking space* in Manhattan may cost $225,000, in London £96,000, in Boston two sold for $560,000. Since the Second World War, including the interstate highway system, the United States has spent close to $3 trillion on road construction and repair.[9] Why are $1,500 speed bumps difficult to stomach as inconvenient and somehow costly?

The fact that we build roads in national parks and wildlife preserves requires a Latourian rest stop to add another actor who contributes to their materiality: wildlife. Permitting automobiles in national parks requires the introduction of special expensive roadways, "wildlife crossing structures" (WCS), to enable migrating or simply passing animals to get to the other side of the road. In East African parks, the authorities are limited to such low-cost approaches to protect animals as signs, WCS, and speed bumps, both because of their cost and because of absence of police personnel in parks.[10] Why did the megafauna cross the road? A speed bump enabled them.

6 SPEED BUMPOLOGY

Speed bumps and traffic calming as scientific fields received great impetus from research, insurance, and other organizations, and from legislation that specified targets and standards for automobile, road, and pedestrian safety; in this way, the speed bump is, as Thomas Hughes elaborated, a large-scale technological system—physical components, natural resources, and organizations that interact with other artifacts.[1] Among the leaders in research on automobile and road safety are the Insurance Institute for Highway Safety, the National Highway Traffic and Safety Administration, and the Dutch Institute for Road Safety Research (SMOV). Founded in the 1960s, SMOV pioneered research on alcohol impairment, pedestrian behavior, guardrails, headlamps, and scores of other issues, and has published tens of thousands of reports, short papers, and studies annually.

In the 1960s SMOV's major concerns were glare, street lighting, alcohol, and tunnels. Studies on lighting were not surprising, both for reasons of safety and because of the close relationship between industry and research. The presence of Philips Electric in Eindhoven with its ties to the Technical

University meant a variety of studies on, for example, automobile headlights.[2] In the 1970s SMOV researchers continued to focus on lighting (rear lighting in automobiles and easy-to-read controls for the driver) and alcohol, but also turned to ways to slow traffic, to identify accident correlations, and a vigorous effort to protect pedestrians and cyclists.

Early on, SMOV specialists analyzed data regarding automobile accidents, morbidity, and safety using a comparative, international approach. The analysis revealed significant and growing public health problems: Were some countries less safe and why? Were the statistics comparable? One specialist looked at the number of accidents per 10,000; population death rate; accidents per 10,000 motor vehicles; accidents per 10,000,000 kilometers driven; and so on. In the mid-1960s rates were higher in Europe than in the United States, but rising in the United States because of new drivers, increased travel, more small cars, and higher speeds. Worryingly, the number of deaths in accidents increased more rapidly than the number of inhabitants, and there were significant differences in deaths per kilometers traveled, with the United States the lowest and Belgium and Italy the highest.[3]

The Dutch also pioneered crash test research. The Research Institute for Road Vehicles TNO, part of the Organization for Industrial Research, has several facilities for full-scale crash tests and to check compliance with standards of seat belts, crash helmets, child restraint systems, and the like. SWOV has its own program for crash tests regarding roadside obstacles and crash barriers. This research contributed to the passage of auto seat belt and moped and motorcycle helmet laws in the 1970s that, along with less driving, led to declines in accident fatalities and injuries.[4]

In the United States several public and private bodies engage the issue of automobile safety. The Insurance Institute for Highway Safety, perhaps out of self-interest, has pushed the development of the field. It sought to lower insurance payouts for damage to property, injuries, and fatalities. Founded in 1959 by three major insurance associations representing 80 percent of the US auto insurance market, at first it supported research contracts. But in the late 1960s, "IIHS was reinvented as an independent research organization," under William Haddon Jr., a doctor "who served as the nation's first federal highway safety chief." Haddon transformed the highway safety field "from one focused solely on crash prevention to one using a modern, scientific approach to identify a full range of options for reducing crash losses." This led to focus not only on human factors (age, impairment, fatigue, seat belts) but also on crash avoidance, crashworthiness, roadway designs, and safety. The institute has had great success with fatality rate reduction even as the population and the number of miles driven have climbed, mostly a result of safer vehicles and roads.[5]

The US Transportation Research Board was established in 1920 to exchange information and research results about highway technology. Renamed the Highway Research

Board (HRB) in 1925, its members established standing committees, publications, and held an annual meeting. In the 1950s HRB expanded efforts to include management of ad hoc research projects. As the Transportation Research Board from 1974, it has turned to conducting policy studies and managing research. As one of six major divisions of the National Research Council, a private, nonprofit institution, the TRB gets funding from state and federal agencies.[6]

Another contributor to speed bumpology, AASHTO, the Association of State Highway Traffic Officials, seeks "to foster the development, operation, and maintenance of an integrated national transportation system."[7] Its functions include lobbying when it serves as liaison between state departments of transportation and the federal government. It sets technical standards for all phases of highway system development—including speed bumps. AASHTO publications run the gamut from geometric design of roads and highways (the AASHTO "Green Book"), bridges, pavement design, management and friction, lighting, hot-mix asphalt paving, draining, cost estimation guides, rights-of-way and construction, vegetation, sustainable roads, outsourcing, and speed bumps.[8]

The Institute of Transportation Engineers, an international educational and scientific association, focuses on mobility and safety needs. ITE members apply technology and scientific principles to research, planning, design, implementation, operation, and development for any mode of ground transportation. Founded in 1930, ITE has grown to 17,000 members in more than 90 countries who have moved from questions of accidents and congestion in the 1920s to the creation of a profession whose members assist local, municipal, and state governments in dealing with traffic problems, safety, road design, signage, and so on.[9] The institute publishes the *ITE Journal* (in 2015 reaching 85 volumes). The leading journal of the field, judging by citation indices, is the international *Transportation Science* (1967–present) for an audience that includes academics applying quantitative approaches to transportation and practitioners who work on problems in supply chain management, logistic, aviation, railroads, highways traffic, public transportation, and military transport. Yet there is little to speak of on traffic calming or speed bumps, although the editor points out that "the focus of the journal is on the design and operation of transport systems, which is somewhat different."[10] Still, the fact that none of these journals really addresses traffic calming as a regular topic or offers it as a general rubric indicates that traffic calming does not attract specialists in leading journals.

We are more likely to encounter discussions of traffic calming at ITE conference presentations. At the annual meeting in Kissimmee, Florida, in March 1999, two researchers warned of a potential "backlash" to traffic calming, even as it solved the problem of community neighborhood roads becoming "awash" in traffic—this only two years after the ITE selected "calming" as the "Hot Topic of 1997." The backlash consisted of petitions to ban speed humps in Maryland, through a judge's order to remove speed "tables" in Florida, to the removal of speed humps and traffic circles in California.[11] This suggests ITE members have technocratic approach to calming—the belief that technology itself may solve problems, but that social and political issues of *Verkehrsberuhigung* are not crucial in their calculations. In any event, many speed hump/bump designs are based on such ITE publications as *Guidelines for the Design and Application of Speed Humps* (May 1993).

In the 1960s, specialists turned systematically to the study of pedestrian safety—to fatality and injury rates and their severity—to provide an empirical foundation effort to pursue traffic calming. These experts in the new field of automobile safety, concentrated in northern Europe and the United States, and especially in the Netherlands, expanded focus of this research to transform city sidewalks and neighborhoods into safer spaces. A number of OECD studies established the relationship between the existence of pedestrian technologies (zebra crossings [painted crosswalks], signal controlled crossings, and grade separated crossings) and the relative risk to pedestrians in the act of crossing. Generally, the studies showed reduced risk with well-marked crossings,[12] but the researchers had not yet recognized traffic-calming technologies as well; instead they continued to see the need to move traffic, not calm it. They were concerned how to "modify" pedestrian and driver behavior toward the ends of increasing safety. A later fan of the *woonerf*, the Dutch sociologist Kraay, argued that it was difficult to modify pedestrian behavior in "conflicts" with wheeled traffic, and that technologies, laws, and educational campaigns were not necessarily of benefit. He suggested that only physical segregation of motorized traffic from pedestrians in entire neighborhoods was of unquestionable benefit, but isolation was also very costly.[13]

How did we decide that 30 kilometers/hour is a crucial metric for automobile safety—with or without speed bumps? In 1979 Ashton and Mackay established the fact that the chances of survival of a pedestrian-car collision at speeds greater than 30 kilometers/hour were small, and of course also dependent on age (a child, being smaller, and being struck by a vehicle in the head or upper torso would much more likely face life-threatening injuries than an adult in the same crash). They understood that bumper design could play a role in reducing risk. "The location of the bumper not only determines the location of the fracture but also appears to influence the likelihood of a fracture occurring as a result of bumper contact," they wrote. Pelvic fractures occurred more frequently with vehicles having short bumper leads than with vehicles having long bumper leads.[14] If standard bumper heights and designs would help, then manufacturers oppose the idea since they sell on style and looks, and also claim higher costs when required to meet new safety standards.[15]

Reducing speed thus has long been established as the golden path to safety. A speed limit of 30 kilometers/hour reinforces the physical limitation of speed by the speed bump and other proven traffic-calming measures. It results in a significant reduction in injury accidents by 22 percent (± 13%). It lowers the speed of motorized traffic, discourages through traffic, improves traffic safety both through accident reduction and diminishing the threat posed by traffic, and it reduces such traffic "nuisances" as parking congestion, noise, and other pollution, while promoting the mobility of cyclists and pedestrians.[16]

7 CRASHWORTHY AUTOMOBILES AS SPEED BUMPS

It has always been hard to argue with the automobile. Prosperity and the future welfare of the nation were connected with the automobile, as were freedom and democracy. In his message to the US Congress on April 12, 1921, President Warren Harding wrote, "The highways are not only feeders to the railroads and afford relief from their burdens; they are actually lines of motor traffic in interstate commerce. They are the smaller arteries of the larger portion of our commerce, and the motor car has become an indispensable instrument in our political, social and industrial life."[1] Harding could not have known how this "indispensable instrument" would have tremendous public health, infrastructure, and other costs. But his infatuation with automobiles was widely shared.

America became the center of automobiles and automobility with 460,000 cars in 1910, 1.7 million in 1914, 4.8 million registered cars and trucks in the United States in 1919 versus

720,000 for the rest of the world, and over 1,000 different manufacturers. Yet by 1929 there were as many fatalities from automobiles as from homicides and suicides together: 31,500 deaths in all, 13 percent higher than in 1928. The millions of automobiles had "infested the country and with them the mortality since 1910 rose nearly 1,000%." The automobile was a "growing menace." A specialist in public health law, James Tobey, observed that traffic regulations and educational campaigns had failed to deliver safety improvements, while mortality from autos had risen so that only about ten diseases combined caused more deaths. Tobey blamed the "human element." He claimed, "The careless, the arrogant, the unfit, the unbalanced, and the drunken driver are at fault in most instances." He called for more stringent requirements to judge the fitness of drivers with a medical examination, training requirements, and strict enforcement of reasonable licensing.[2] Two University of Chicago scholars shared Tobey's view, calling the car "an instrument of injury and death"[3] It would be half a century before policy makers and spokespeople for the auto industry absolved the driver of his "arrogance" and admitted that the automobile required radical safety re-engineering. Decades later, speed bumps would slow it on the roads, while "crashworthiness" would ensure greater safety within.

Such individuals as plastic surgeon Claire Straith and lawyer Ralph Nader called attention to safety issues in design of automobiles and roadways. Straith, a Detroit plastic surgeon, specialized in reconstructing the faces and skulls of automobile accident victims. He recognized that the hard steel interiors of automobiles—their knobs, handles and other protrusions—and their glass contributed significantly to injury and death. He actively sought seat belts as standard in automobiles. He installed lap belts in his own cars, and he designed and patented a dashboard crash pad. Disturbed by the injured whose facial scars he had had to treat, Straith wrote widely about automobile safety. He noted, "In its relatively short career, the motor car has already brought about more casualties in the United States than all the wars in which this country has been engaged. In 1935 alone, motor car accidents caused approximately 36,000 deaths and a far greater number of severe injuries."[4] Straith wrote directly to Walter P. Chrysler and called on his company to introduce such safety improvements as belts and padded dashboards. Chrysler did not do this, but did introduce "recessed knobs, rubber buttons, curving door handles that could not snag motorists, and padded seat tops."[5]

The absolute number of annual fatalities and the number per 100,000 population rose rapidly and steadily through the 1960s. By the time Ralph Nader published *Unsafe at Any Speed* in 1964, in which he documented the inherent "unsafety" of the General Motors rear engine Corvair, 46,000 Americans perished annually in automobile accidents, and by 1972, the peak year, 55,000. By 2015, without changes in automobile and traffic safety, the carnage might have reached 100,000 fatalities annually, rivaled in "unnatural" deaths only by smoking (480,000), drug overdoses (46,000), and guns (33,000).

Traffic safety improvements within the vehicle and on the roadways came slowly. One of the reasons for the rush-hour-like hesitation to seek improvements was the philosophical battle over the accident-proneness of drivers and pedestrians and their responsibility for inevitable accidents. Manufacturers feared findings of their liability for design flaws (which they always contended was close to null, as cigarette manufacturers tried to blame the consumer for getting lung cancer by smoking[6]). They preferred to find fault with drivers. Another concern was the libertarian worry of the extent to which the state had adopted paternalistic or caretaker status to protect foolish, drunk, accident-prone, or otherwise guilty accident victims, or to prevent freedom of choice among adults *not* to wear seat belts or helmets. Consumers paid the price of delay because manufacturers hesitated to add safety devices also because of expense; they reasoned that any safety additions would increase the overall cost of the automobile and lead consumers to purchase fewer "luxury" options from which they generated higher profits.

A final problem was that it took decades before policy makers, engineers, city planners, traffic specialists, and others to accept the fact that there would be crashes, that vehicles had to be made crashworthy, and that cyclists and pedestrians had to be protected. One of the confusions was the fact that quite often it takes some time before sufficient data have accumulated to understand patterns and causalities. For example, hundreds of people died and were injured in jet ski, snowmobile, and ATV accidents in the United States in the 1970s, 1980s, and 1990s, before local, state, and federal officials noticed the epidemiology of the injuries that was connected with their use. In one particular case, hapless recreationists on jet skis who fell off them suffered high-energy enemas that left them hospitalized or bleeding to death with "rectal blowout"—a phenomenon reported in the *Journal of Trauma* in 1999.[7]

8 RACE, EQUALITY, AND TRAFFIC

On April 5, 1962, President Kennedy submitted a message to Congress on "The Transportation System of our Nation" in which he claimed, "An efficient and dynamic transportation system is vital to our domestic economic growth, productivity, and progress. Affecting the cost of every commodity we consume or export, it is equally vital to our ability to compete abroad. It influences both the cost and flexibility of our defense preparedness, and both the business and recreational opportunities of our citizens." He offered no speed bumps. Government policy had to ensure "the availability of the fast, safe and economical transportation services" in order "to move people and goods, without waste or discrimination, in response to private and public demands at the lowest cost consistent with health, convenience, national security and other broad public objectives." Kennedy called for research into issues of urban transportation and recommended long-range federal financial and technical assistance. Yet Kennedy worried that urban renewal and highway projects were leading to the removal of 15,000 families and 1,500 businesses each year, and that these people and businesses required assistance.[1]

Indeed the automobile, like dams and other large-scale technologies, has led to ousting of huge numbers of people around the world from their homes and the destruction of their neighborhoods and homes in the name of progress, speed, efficiency, and the public good. Traffic abatement suggests we are willing to push people aside to convenience the automobile, but unwilling to adopt cost-effective safety and environmental measures to convenience the pedestrian and strengthen the neighborhood. In the United States, a juggernaut of construction spread ribbons of asphalt and concrete from Maine to Florida and from New York to California as poor folk and people of color suffered the greatest losses of home and heritage.

It's my impression that there are fewer speed bumps in lower income neighborhoods than in high-income neighborhoods where residents tend to be white. Modern dirt and gravel, asphalt, and concrete roads have been inherently political from the start, from their service to big businesses in forestry, to their embrace as crucial to commerce, to the construction of rights-of-way through poor neighbors, to their facilitation of flight from inner cities and the establishment of concrete bands ("beltways") that separate suburbia from those cities. And recall Robert Moses's racist parkway design.

It's not only my impression; indeed race and class remain critical elements of automobile safety. While motor vehicle accident mortality has declined overall, the larger decreases are among more highly educated individuals, while there have been mortality increases among the least educated, and socioeconomic differences in motor vehicle accident mortality have worsened over time. Some of the reasons may be the decline in the number of trauma centers in poor and rural communities, roads in poor conditions in these communities, and fewer (if any) crosswalks over major roads. Similarly, the poor residents may have "less political power to fight for design improvements like stop signs, sidewalks and speed bumps." This occurs throughout the world: the poor disproportionately bear the costs of automobility.[2]

President Lyndon Johnson was committed to civil rights for African Americans and other minorities. He pushed the passage of the Civil Rights Act of 1964 and ordered the federal government to support its enforcement. Yet he encountered challenges in seeing to it that the construction of the Interstate System proceeded with race in mind. His chief of the Bureau of Public Roads assumed that "in revitalizing cities and encouraging suburbanization the highways could not help but benefit 'fringe' members of society. 'Slum-clearance projects' would revitalize blighted streets once traffic moved to the interstate, accelerate commerce, and create jobs." The costly right-of-way acquisition practices that displaced so many poor folk—many of them African American—hardly contributed to revitalization of their lives.[3]

In high school I worked part-time for a Pittsburgh engineering firm that conducted right-of-way work for the Commonwealth of Pennsylvania. We inventoried a property at businesses scheduled for demolition to make way for new interstates. The chief engineer tabulated how much the Commonwealth should offer a business to leave a site in the right-of-way. I recall visiting several meatpacking plants in Philadelphia whose operations led me to abandon hotdogs cold turkey. Federal, state, and national government may take private property through their power of eminent domain if they provide "adequate compensation" to the owner of the property to be taken. The government must prove that taking for the public good ensures the common good and the benefit of the public in terms of health and safety. Yet in these cases they took property to benefit the automobile, evicted people from their homes, and provided modest compensation—and traffic—in exchange. As Joni Mitchell noted, they "paved paradise and they put up a parking lot," literally in my town of Waterville, Maine.

At the beginning of the 1960s passenger trains disappeared from Waterville when Interstate 95, some 3 kilometers north of downtown, was completed; the cheaper land near the highway also drew stores and fast food joints. The city's Urban Renewal Authority was determined to rejuvenate downtown. It took advantage of federal largesse to demolish old—including historic—houses, churches, and hotels to improve traffic flow and draw automobiles back in the way that I-95 had siphoned them off. The authority razed a working class neighborhood behind Main Street, pushing aside mill workers for a massive parking lot that was supposed to be a magnet for shoppers.[4] Locals call what happened "Urban Removal."

In 2007 I met with the then mayor of Waterville, the notorious Paul LePage, governor of Maine, to discuss the relationship with its sister city, Kotlas, Russia. I steered the conversation toward traffic and the question of revitalizing Waterville's downtown by turning Main Street into a pedestrian mall, and routing vehicles through the parking lot—or as it was anointed, the Grand Concourse—utilizing unused parking spaces for a street adorned with greenery, with brick walkways and benches, and with speed bumps to slow the traffic. While the former Hathaway Shirt Factory has been turned into condominiums with high ceilings and wonderful views, the other mills have shuttered, the Franco-American and Lebanese neighborhoods have aged, and the city center remains as LePage left it, with one-way streets and dangerous and blind front-in parking that barely slows drivers otherwise intent in getting out of town.

9 PEDESTRIAN MALLS AS LARGE-SCALE SPEED BUMPS

Ah, the joy of pedestrian malls, of walking through the center of a European city, free of automobiles, with stores and restaurants and parks, curiosities, historical buildings, museums, opera houses—all within a few moments of each other! These malls are car-free zones where street space is reserved for pedestrian use but permits delivery trucks and street cleaning vehicles to service businesses during the early morning. If pedestrian malls are common in European cities, then they are rarely found in the United States. US cities installed approximately two hundred pedestrian malls before the end of the twentieth century, but only about fifteen remain in use today. The revitalization of inner cities and shopping areas requires precisely more malls since "sustainable urbanism" must rely upon reduced auto dependence and increased pedestrian activity. The pedestrian mall—a large-scale traffic-calming technology par excellence—enhances the quality of life, livability, and sustainability of cities.[1]

North European cities have been working at traffic calming since the end of the Second World War when pedestrian malls began to appear. The first of them were simple and, to some architectural critics, uninspiring in style. Builders used prefabricated concrete paving blocks and planters to keep costs down. But the zones worked well in attracting pedestrians. Sadly, war on civilians enabled the rise of the

FIGURE 6 "Munich's Fussgangerzone (Pedestrian Mall) prohibits automobiles, buses and bicycles, and has done much to revitalize the city's commercial and Cultural Center," September 1973.
Courtesy of Yoichi R. (Yoichi Robert) Okamoto, US National Archives and Records Administration, Collection of Environmental Protection Agency, NWDNS-412-DA-9310.

pedestrian mall. A British bombing raid in 1943 destroyed 80 percent of Kassel, Germany, whose postwar leaders determined to build a mall to bring people back to their shops and businesses. The mall opened in 1953 to great fanfare and success. Kassel was not alone; dozens of cities repeated the experience and often used similar, mass-produced brick, stone, and pavers, and with a similar contribution to German recovery from the war, while keeping the auto at bay.[2]

The Lijnbaan, in Rotterdam, Holland, opened in 1953, remains "the busiest shopping street in the greater Rotterdam area."[3] Lijnbaan, too, was a postwar reconstruction project to remove the automobile from the equation better to integrate cities with pedestrians and their activities. "Instead of shops with apartments above on either side of a roadway, shops are located on pedestrians only streets like the later shopping malls," one description notes. The broad Lijnbaan is 12 to 18 meters wide, and uses planters, sculptures, and initially also aviaries, with sun and rain canopies "as a transition between interior and exterior."[4]

In Copenhagen, "Strøget" indicates that an entire neighborhood might be set aside from the automobile. At the beginning of the 1960s, as higher volume automobile traffic overwhelmed Copenhagen's narrow old streets, the city council voted to establish a pedestrian zone from Town Hall Square in the west to Kongens Nytorv (King's New Square) in the Strøget section with its "maze of small streets and historical squares" to a total length of 3.2 kilometers. After a two-year trial period, the council voted to transform the zone—"with much cleaner air—and no traffic—plus many happy pedestrians" into a permanent architecture.[5]

The power of the automobile prevented the pedestrian mall from much success in America, although many cities attempted to build magnets for shoppers and businesses in city centers. Urban retailing reached its peak in the 1920s—and has declined ever since because of the automobile. When suburbs became the magnet for the middle class, downtowns began an even more rapid decline. Between 1959 and the early 1980s, "more than 200 American cities closed part of their downtown street networks to vehicles" to compete with suburban shopping malls. But the pedestrians went to malls anyway, even if it meant driving to some distant eyesore of box stores and mass-produced consumerism. In the 1980s such mega-boxes as Home Depot, Target, and especially Walmart came to dominate the consumer sales business. They have persuaded municipalities to support the construction of new access roads and parking lots for them at taxpayer expense that created bottlenecks at peak traffic. Few pedestrian malls remain except in university towns or near tourist centers.[6]

The appearance of body-painted, topless women in Times Square, New York, who earn money by posing with tourists in photos, led New York officials to consider tearing up Times Square and other new pedestrian plazas to end what they see as vulgar practices. There are speed bumps for vulgarity, too: requirements for pasties and limitations for the performers to evening hours of work. From the point of view of traffic calming, human safety, and the reclaiming of public space from the automobile, ripping up pedestrian areas there would be the worst thing to do. Indeed the "pedestrianization" of Times Square led injury rates to decline, traffic flow in central Manhattan to improve, and local business to thrive.[7]

The European approach to calming begins with the premise that pedestrians come first and automobiles much later. Planners and residents of Trondheim, Norway, a coastal city of 183,000 residents, turned the city center into a pedestrian area while minimizing motorized traffic though low-tech obstacles, fines, and tariffs. Most of the residents live uphill or along the fjords and journey to city center for work or play along roads whose speed limits were reduced to 30 kilometers/hour, with speed bumps and traffic cameras to ensure compliance with the law, and with excellent bus service, high gasoline taxes, and bicycle lanes as added incentives to avoid automobility.

10 THE *WOONERF*: THE NEIGHBORHOOD SPEED BUMP

Dense population and traffic circulation require proactive measures. The Netherlands has 15 million people, or 350 inhabitants per kilometer^2; Dutch citizens own more than 5.7 million passenger cars, 12 million bicycles, almost 500,000 mopeds, and 180,000 motorcycles. The Dutch transport total network includes 103,000 kilometers of road, of which 47,500 kilometers are streets and roads inside built-up areas. Yet by attacking the automobile as a problem, not only a convenience or necessity, the Dutch reduced traffic fatalities over a twenty-year period from 3,300 in 1972 to 1,300 in 1992 at the same time as mobility doubled. First, planners noted that the majority of traffic accident injuries and fatalities inside built-up areas took place on traffic arteries: those streets or roads where traffic or flow function dominates. *Woonerfs* radically reduced accidents because they separated residential areas from traffic functions that "do not tolerate each other well."[1]

With community effort, pressure on politicians, a realistic understanding of the impacts of automobiles on the quality of life, and a willingness to allocate funds, entire neighborhoods can become speed bumps. Neighborhoods are—or should be—places of home life, children at play, dogs on leashes, parents with strollers, schools and small shops, and not thoroughfares for automobiles. Planners and engineers can create them with designs that calm roadways and emphasize pedestrian activities. They can narrow roads, make one-way streets, raise crosswalks, and install speed humps. These neighborhoods embrace a human aesthetic that emphasizes illumination, ventilation, quiet, greenery, and playgrounds, not speed, vrooming sounds, smoke, and broad thoroughfares. The Dutch pioneered this approach in the *woonerf*.

Called "the most celebrated Dutch contribution to urban environmental traffic management," the living neighborhood that is a residence, meeting place, playground, and walking area originated in a 1975 report from the Netherlands Association of Local Authorities (VNG). Tried first in Delft, Emmen, Rijswijk, and Eindhoven, it was subsequently applied widely across Holland in 4,000 neighborhoods, and embraced not only shopping regions but also entire residential areas. The *woonerf* discourages motorized traffic and admits only destination traffic that is secondary to other road users and at speeds of a walking pace (or approximately

5–8 kilometers/hour). The *woonerf* succeeded because planners recognized that it was only "part of a whole package of measures—including the design of the urban traffic environment, legislation and law enforcement, information and training—to influence driver behavior and thus improve both road safety and the quality of life, which have been under study in the Netherlands in recent years."[2]

While also accessible to motorists and cyclists or mopeds, the *woonerf* design prevents motorized traffic from moving through the area, by avoiding conventional straight pavements and curbs. To protect pedestrians and playing children, designers use physical and visual facilities (narrow passages, trees, bollards, varied paving) to induce motorized traffic to enter the area at a low speed and continue to drive slowly.[3] Thus, the *woonerf* is a massive speed bump with the speed of wheeled traffic derived from the design, not the other way around.

Costs, physical space requirements, and other factors have limited the construction of *woonerf*s. Some people criticize them because of the difficulties they have in recognizing entries and exits: the roads from which cars from *woonerf*s enter traffic are sometimes blind or have speed humps from which cars might roll into oncoming traffic.[4] Some *woonerf* neighborhoods have inadequate facilities for handicapped people. The *woonerf* can be costly since it requires the reconstruction of streets, and removal of curbs and some sidewalks to achieve common shared spaces for pedestrians and their strollers, children, pets, and bicycles; these costs are several times higher per square meter than those for simply more pavement.[5] As a result, the *woonerf* often remained restricted to relatively small areas, and many Dutch residents actually found the early *woonerf* less attractive because "pedestrians . . . are more or less compelled to zigzag across the street by obstacles built on one side or the other. This makes them cross through moving traffic at points with poor visibility."[6] Yet they are mostly popular, although children, elderly people, and mothers with children seem to be more positive in the like of the *woonerf* than people who prefer traditional residential areas. Resistance is most common among nonresidents, that is, those who lack knowledge about their purposes. But there is no doubt that *woonerven* are safer that other neighborhoods.[7]

11 TAMING ROADS THEMSELVES

They paved paradise, and put up a parking lot.
—JONI MITCHELL

Improvements in road safety accompanied those for the automobile, and contributed to an environment of acceptance for the speed bump. They included better geometries, new surfaces, improved treatment of road hazards, better medians, and Jersey barriers. At first engineers directed road improvements toward achieving higher vehicle speeds. As more and more vehicles filled roads and highways, it became necessary to engineer roads for safety, too, with such modest technological features as guardrails; rumble strips; banked curves; snap-off signs; and improved lighting, all to minimize the likelihood of head-on collisions between two or more vehicles and the odds of striking an off-road object. Meteorological factors, of course, contributed to accidents; wet road surfaces had an impact on general visibility, increased glare, obscured markings and signs, and reduced tire/road surface forces. Several surface technologies offered solutions: grooves, small transverse discharge channels, synthetic resin surface treatments, and porous asphaltic concrete all were possible.[1] Of course, the safest and cheapest tactic would be for drivers to slow their speed in inclement weather.

In 1969 a member of the American Bar Association described highway directional and other signs, light poles, poorly designed guardrails, abutments, and trees (originally added to "beautify" the roadway) as "the death penalty" for causing death and injury, being struck time and again, and then rebuilt again and again. The jurist likened this rebuilding without learning as a death sentence and asked why it had not been abolished. Some accidents resulted from stupidity or drunkenness. But, he asked, shouldn't people be given "reasonable opportunity" to regain control of their cars and a chance of survival? And what if the reason for leaving the road was a blowout or other mechanical failure? He blamed engineers and builders of roads, highway commissioners, legislators, and governors who allowed the death traps to remain.[2]

In 1972 "less than a dozen" states were even identifying "hazardous fixed objects" along their highways. The IIHS produced a film *Boobytrap!* that premiered before the US House Public Works Committee and its Chairman Rep. John Blatnik (D-Minn.). Blatnik called the film "a dramatic and compelling motion picture" that "points up most vividly many of the mortal hazards that have unwittingly been built into some of our very newest highways." He asked highway engineers in every state to work toward eliminating "crashes with man-made and natural objects along the highway" and other "booby-traps."[3]

Blatnik himself supported major public works. He secured increased federal funding for sewage treatment, the St. Lawrence Seaway, the Niagara River power project, and the interstate highway system.[4] Blatnik insisted on the need not only for construction but also for safety. In 1968 he wrote:

> It would seem that today's automobile owner never had it so good. His car has air conditioning, stereophonic tapes, disc brakes, peek-a-boo lights, power steering, power windows, power seats, adjustable and telescoping steering post, and a host of other features meant to make his driving more safe and more pleasant. He is able to get into this luxurious palace and drive on superhighways from New York to Chicago without the interference of a single traffic light; soon he can so drive from one end of the country to another. Yet more and more a chill, almost a fear, is supplanting what used to be the sheer pleasure of driving, and a corresponding waning of confidence stealthily creeps in.[5]

That year 53,000 people were killed and 2,000,000 more were injured on highways. Blatnik lamented, "One can hardly blame the motorist for feeling short-changed" because he "had spent thousands of dollars on his car and billions on the roads." Blatnik asked, "Could not all this money have bought him better than the one chance in four that his car would become bloodied in a highway accident?" Blatnik blamed the machine and the roadways for their unsafe designs.[6]

Construction of wider roads and four-lane roads required a scientific approach to median barriers, earthen ditches, and guardrails to give "sufficient separation" between streams of traffic. Evidence showed that when any road reached roughly 60,000 vehicles/day, then barriers became cost-effective, and in any event cars rolled over in medians or off road. At some point in the struggle with traffic, even low volume roads required median strips built to the highest safety standards. Median strips designed at 10–11 meters eventually became standard for many highways.[7]

Proper geometry, a challenge to determine, helped in the design of medians: the narrower the median, the more rigid the structure to be used to prevent penetration, yet not so rigid to cause a vehicle to bounce back into the other lane. When struck, the median must also provide the smallest possible longitudinal decelerations while being easy to repair and low cost.[8] Concrete proved to be the key material, and it was relatively inexpensive, too. At first, swooning under the influence of concrete, engineers rushed to use it, and sought not to slow but to stop vehicles. When they rebuilt signs, they anchored them more fixedly and firmly in concrete. Their guardrails guided vehicles into obstructions. Exits approached too suddenly without giving drivers time to react, and drivers lost control on exiting or were rear-ended in their furious braking.

One of the glories of engineering, if you are a civil engineer, is concrete, and one of the glories of highway construction is the Jersey barrier, a fixed median that can serve also for temporary construction safety detours.[9] While not exactly clear when engineers first used concrete median barriers, they certainly appeared in the mid-1940s "on US-99 on the descent from the Tehachapi Mountains in the central valley south of Bakersfield, California."[10] They have multiplied and, as written in Exodus 1:7, "Became exceedingly mighty, so that the land was filled with them."

The first concrete median barrier used in New Jersey was developed at the Stevens Institute of Technology, in Hoboken, and installed in 1955 at 18 inches tall. It looked like a low vertical wall with a curb on each side. At first, New Jersey did not use crash-testing experiments to develop the barrier; rather the state highway department observed accident results. Both New Jersey and California continued trial-and-error work in the early 1960s, and the Jersey barrier was widely adopted by California; the state installed 132 miles by 1972 and 680 miles by 1988. The barrier has spread to every nation since then like fast food franchises. Operational problems such as vehicle takeoff and turnover led to modification of shape, and the height was increased from 24 inches to 32 inches in 1959, and to the commonly seen shape and size up to 2 meters.[11]

The modern Jersey barrier solves problems of safety. In January 2015 bridge officials shut down the 3.0 kilometer Golden Gate Bridge in San Francisco, California, to install permanent concrete barriers in order to prevent head-on collisions. Previously, only yellow plastic cones kept traffic apart—and there had been 128 head-on collisions, resulting in sixteen deaths. It's hard to find tax money to support public education and school lunch programs, or make them more healthful, but the bridge authorities managed this $30 million project in less than a weekend.[12]

Eventually improvements in smoothing terrain, increasing width of roads, making them skid resistant, employing reflective paint and reflectors,[13] adding rumble strips to alert drivers, making approaches longer and more gradual, building guardrails (and burying the ends, raising the height, and reinforcing for impact), using impact barrels, making signage more visible and with break-off standards— all these things have made roads safer, if only encouraging traffic to increase speed.[14] By the twenty-first century these safety features were adopted in all countries with active safety programs.

Another "speed bump," growing in urban popularity, is the roundabout. Perhaps the *carrefour à gyration* (traffic circle) was a French idea. But planners in Britain embraced it fully, first at Letchworth Garden City in 1909.[15] The roundabout increases flow, slows traffic, and cuts down on injury accidents by 50 percent in comparison with other intersections. The Dutch long ago demonstrated that conversion of intersections to roundabouts reduces crashes and injuries significantly. Intersections have significant numbers of left turn accidents and serious head-on and front-angle collisions. Indeed Dutch experience showed that the risk of accidents is (very) low because of the moderate speeds of all traffic approaching and within the roundabout. Traffic flow quality is also higher.[16] In the Netherlands, following replacement of traditional intersections with roundabouts, the number of accidents fell by nearly 100 percent among cars and pedestrians and 30 percent among cyclists. There were several reasons for this: an end to head-on collisions, simplified pedestrian crossings, and most important a drop in speed by motorized traffic.[17]

The city of Carmel, Indiana, touts itself as the world leader of roundabout engineering, as its experience in abandoning now traditional intersections with traffic lights proves. In a glossy brochure Carmel officials proudly reiterated these "community benefits" of traffic calming, the improved aesthetic landscaping and more green space, and the safer crosswalks for pedestrians and cyclists; significantly increased traffic flow and resultant gasoline savings; and significant cost savings, not to mention lower accident costs.[18]

12 CURB CUTS FOR PEOPLE, ROUNDABOUTS FOR AUTOMOBILES

Can we imagine how mobile society would have become had local, state, and national governments spent on sidewalks with curb cuts rather than focusing on Jersey barriers? The curb cut is a dip in the sidewalk graded down from the top to the road that enables people in wheelchairs and with other disabilities to move about more easily. Second World War veterans first pushed for social, political, and technological change when they returned from the war effort in wheelchairs. In 1945, Jack Fisher of Kalamazoo, Michigan, "a disabled veteran and lawyer," celebrated the fact that "his hometown had just installed the nation's first curb cuts to facilitate travel in the downtown area for wheelchair users and others who couldn't navigate the 6-inch curb heights on downtown sidewalks."[1] From that time, veterans across the nation sought these improvements and support systems as well; in the USSR disabled individuals, including veterans, were hidden and stigmatized, as were virtually all other citizens with any kind of disability, and a ranking system of disabilities appeared that privileged those who might be able to work in some small way.[2]

The curb cut represents traffic calming in its recognition of the rights of all pedestrians to have accessible sidewalks and to cross streets freely and safely. Apparently, curb cuts came to prominence in the 1960s in Berkeley, California, as part of the protest against the University of California for its military contracts to help wage war in Vietnam. Many students, graduate students, and veterans, a number of them with spinal injuries, others with polio and cerebral palsy, insisted on changes to the physical landscape of the campus to give them equal rights to other students. They grew tired of the curbs, the challenges of moving about the hilly terrain, their need to rely on friends for help to be mobile. They embellished antiwar political protest with equal rights protest. In response, in the early 1970s the city built the first planned, wheelchair-accessible route in the United States. According to one source, "After riots that brought the National Guard to town, the City renovated the Telegraph Avenue business district, widening sidewalks in a gesture towards local street life. In keeping with a brand new building code, these renovations included wide, flat curb 'ramps' positioned at the corner of the sidewalk."[3]

Like speed bumps, curb cuts and general accessibility were a long time in coming. Section 504 of the Rehabilitation Act of 1973 and the Education for All Handicapped Children Act of 1974 "foreshadowed significant progress" in the rights of vulnerable Americans. Perhaps the first such complying institution, Georgia State University, undertook the effort in 1965 to make its campus fully accessible for handicapped students, even without federal funds.[4] But in a Reagan-era society more interested in tax cuts than curb cuts, and austerity instead of progress in accessibility, financially strapped local government administrations strove to modify or ignore the acts. Local business leaders and other groups sought to repeal them, especially regarding public transport, as "economically unfeasible"; public transport suffered as well.

According to section 504, "subway systems in cities such as New York, Chicago, Boston, Cleveland and Philadelphia would have to be re-equipped with ramps and elevators to allow disabled individuals access to the trains" and buses would have special lifts. Legislators looked at civil rights for the disabled in terms of "practical economic limits," and local administrators claimed that the legislation to provide "extensive services to a small segment of the population" put "undue strain on their budgets."[5]

Shepherded through Congress by Senator Bob Dole (R-Kansas), a disabled veteran, the Americans with Disabilities Act of 1990 (ADA) reversed this shortsighted trend. The Act provided civil rights protections against discrimination based on disability, required employers to provide reasonable accommodations to employees with disabilities, and imposed accessibility requirements on public accommodations using curb cuts, ramps, elevators, and other technologies. Initially many local and state governments failed to allocate the resources necessary to comply with the law. The turning point seems to have been in deciding *Barden v. Sacramento*, in January 2004, when the federal courts compelled the city to comply with the ADA when undertaking public street improvements—in specific, making sidewalks accessible to persons with disabilities. The city of Sacramento agreed to allocate 20 percent of its annual transportation budget over the next thirty years to make the city's pedestrian rights-of-way accessible.[6]

Yet curb cuts for the disabled hit their own speed bump of ignorance, jingoism, and extremism again in 2012 when Senate Republicans voted to reject a United Nations treaty, modeled on the Americans with Disabilities Act, that banned discrimination against disabled people, because it "would infringe on American sovereignty." They insulted Senator Bob Dole, now retired and in a wheelchair, who journeyed to Capitol Hill to remind his former colleagues to be reasonable.[7] Within the United States, ADA progress has been slow; in NYC, a leader in promoting the rights of the disabled, only roughly 10 percent of curb cuts were fully compliant with the ADA by the summer 2015.[8] Some human traffic thus still labors to move about with dignity and equality.

13 THE BICYCLE AS A NEO-LUDDITE TRAFFIC SOLUTION

If only planners throughout the world pursued bicycle-friendly infrastructure to inform the world's drivers both of the need to slow down and of the benefits of commuting to work by human power. The commitment to the bicycle and public transportation has lagged in many places under the assault of the automobile, especially in Anglo-American countries where people rarely cycle or walk, although walking everywhere has declined as a mode of travel—except in the Netherlands.

At one time Americans were world leaders in cycling. In the 1880s they founded the League of American Wheelmen that had 150,000 members by 1900. Los Angeles, the city of automobiles, traffic jams, and slow moving angels, had a dedicated bike highway at the time. In 2015, of US cities only Minneapolis, Minnesota, remained in the world's top twenty bicycle-friendly cities. Americans spend instead an average of nearly one hour each day in their cars commuting round trip.[1]

Country	Cycling	Walking	Total
US	1	10	11
Germany	10	25	35
Netherlands	26	20	46
France*	3	22	25
United Kingdom*	2	22	24
Denmark	20	16	36

FIGURE 7 Cycling and Walking, Percent of Daily Trips, Averaged 1970s–2009.
Adapted from Ralph Buehler and John Pucher, "Walking and Cycling in Western Europe and the United States," TR News, no. 280 (May–June 2012), p. 35.
*Sharp decline in France and the United Kingdom from nearly half the population engaging in daily walking trips in 1970s to 22 percent presently.

Bible reading seems to increase automobile use: the percentage of people who walk or bike to work is lowest in Bible Belt states, and highest in the Northern Rockies and Plains states, NY, PA, Vermont, and Massachusetts, and on the west coast.[2] Of course, the longer the commute, the higher the levels of obesity, cholesterol, pain, fatigue, and anxiety. This does not mean that Bible reading leads to obesity and fatigue, nor does a long commute necessarily mean poor health or poor health habits. The Dutch people on average spend one and a half hours en route every day, longer than the average time for citizens of sixteen EU countries. The Netherlands has at 92 percent the highest percentage of the total population traveling daily and France has, at 72 percent, the lowest percentage.[3] But they bike.

FIGURE 8 "Road For Bicycles in Amsterdam, the Netherlands,"
March 27, 2008.
https://commons.wikimedia.org/wiki/File:Road_for_bicycles_
Amsterdam_01.JPG as accessed July 15, 2016.

Paradoxically, the low rates of walking and cycling in the
United States may contribute to the significantly higher rates
of cyclists killed and injured per 10 million kilometers cycled
and walked, versus the Netherlands, Denmark, Germany,

and the United Kingdom. On top of this, fatality rates fell much less in the United States between the 1970s and 2008 than in other countries,[4] because of inattention to calming.

How can officials slow vehicles to protect increasing numbers of cyclists and pedestrians? By the 1970s traffic safety planners understood that they could not decouple planning measures for improving the traffic safety of automobiles from those for cyclists and pedestrians. One specialist argued that changes in the traffic system had an impact on almost all aspects of society—the sociocultural and economic systems, the physical environment, and the planning system, and whether they considered built-up areas, town centers, or rural regions, they had to treat these things as tightly related.[5] Building on these issues, Danish, German, and Dutch transportation policies have emphasized improvements in the infrastructure for walking and cycling any time they undertake road repairs. For pedestrians, this means auto-free zones in the city center; wide, well-lit sidewalks on every street; pedestrian "refuge islands" for crossing wide streets; clearly marked crosswalks, often raised and with special lighting; "automobiles-must-yield-to-pedestrians" signs at crosswalks; and pedestrian signals at intersections and mid-block crosswalks with ample crossing times.[6] European bikeway systems serve "practical destinations for everyday travel." They help people get to work, school, and places of business. By comparison, most separate bike paths in the United States are located in parks or along rivers, lakes, or harbors and are mainly for recreation.[7] Dedicated bikeways in the United States exist usually only in university towns or other places one might characterize as having "progressive" politics—Portland, Oregon, Seattle, Washington, Cambridge, Massachusetts, and others. Elsewhere, US biking remains fringe, and in France and the United Kingdom its use is rapidly losing out to the automobile.[8]

14 GENDERED SPEED BUMPS

Once there was this kid who
Got into an accident and couldn't come to school
But when he finally came back
His hair had turned from black into bright white
He said that it was from when
The car had smashed so hard

—CRASH TEST DUMMIES, "MMM MMM MMM" (1993)

Why must we calm traffic? What are the dangers of excessive speed? How does the human body react to unnaturally fast decelerations and unexpected impacts with moving or stationary objects—accidents, as we call them? What happens if we do not wear seat belts, get knocked about, or even ejected from an automobile in an accident? We know precisely from the study of accidents (unfortunately often postmortem study), and also from clinical tests using cadavers and crash test dummies. Specialists have used cadavers for centuries in morbidly fascinating research on the limits of the human body; ancient dissectionists posited the uterus had horns. The value of human cadaveric subjects in injury biomechanics research from the 1960s to the 1990s must be tens of thousands of lives saved and countless injuries prevented.[1]

Specialists at Wayne State University outside of Detroit, Michigan, first collected data on the effects of high-speed collisions on the human body in the 1930s. They contributed to the development of crash biomechanics by using human cadavers. They dropped ball bearings on skulls, dumped bodies down elevator shafts, and strapped corpses in automobiles and crashed them. Our sensitivities, our cadaver shortages, and our military and space programs led us to the crash test dummy, although scientists also used chimpanzees, bears, pigs, and other animals in the growing series of tests.

Like many other technologies and management systems that grew out of military innovation—the American system of mass production, Taylorism, the computer and radio, solid state electronics, and so on[2]—the shift to crash test dummies from cadavers owes a great deal to the US aeronautics and space program during the Cold War. Crash test dummies were developed in 1949 under an Air Force contract to test ejection seats, helmets, and G- and other forces. The first dummies were lifelike in size and weight, but rigid and otherwise rather mechanical; the next dummies used imbedded sensors to measure acceleration and the force of impact, and their spines and skins were more lifelike.[3] The Air Force underwrote a research project at UCLA in the 1950s to study automobile collisions with the hope of saving "up to 20,000 lives a year."[4] Of course, their research was intended to benefit military aeronautics and space programs.

By the mid-1950s automotive companies had begun their own crash testing with in-house dummies—for example, Ford's Ferd I and Ferd II that contributed to the design of "collapsing steering wheels, padded dashboards, doors that will not open in a collision, shatter-proof rearview mirrors, and padded sun visors."[5] In the mid-1960s, in response to increased federal pressure for higher safety standards, and with the creation of the federal National Highway Transportation Safety Administration, the automotive industry became more active in crash test dummy development. GM's Hybrid I and Hybrid II, that met the American Federal Motor Vehicle Safety Standard (FMVSS) of 1972 for testing seat belts, came next.

The IIHS Vehicle Research Center joined the dummy research effort to explore front, side, and angle crashes. The dummies ranged in size from a six-month-old infant to a ninety-fifth-percentile man. Contemporary dummies cost about $200,000 each, have articulating vertebrae and other realistic features, and use make-up (grease paint) to help determine dummy contact points. They have sensors that measure forces—acceleration and deceleration against values of stress and strain "known to exceed the strength of human bones and tissues to determine how a real person might be injured."[6]

The dummies were essentially male-gendered to exclude a series of important questions about safety; Stanford researchers pointed out how crucial this oversight was to the safety question. They observed that a "women's normal seated position differed from what was defined as the standard seating position." Women sit closer to the steering column because they tend to be shorter and therefore are at greater risk for injury in a frontal collision. (For decades most medical, clinical, and other studies similarly excluded women by considering the male as the standard.) The introduction of seat belts and their mandatory use led many people to assume that both "mother and fetus were safer with a standard three-point seat belt than with no seat belt."[7] Yet the absence of any research made such a conclusion premature; anecdotal evidence indicated that seat belts as presently designed might even be hazardous to the fetus even when the pregnant woman was not injured.[8] Ultimately researchers concluded that pregnant women should use the three-point seat belt, although those women who carried low were at risk if the seat belt rode up on the pregnant belly in a crash. Researchers in the United States and Europe introduced the pregnant crash test dummy in the 1990s, as well as new software, following the lead of Volvo that in 2002 developed a virtual pregnant crash dummy, "Linda."[9]

15 IF STOPPED IN TRAFFIC, HOPE FOR A CRASHWORTHY AUTOMOBILE

In 1972, while a student at Antioch College in a cooperative education program, I worked at the Center for Auto Safety created by Ralph Nader to tackle the growing problem of automobile fatalities and injuries. The Center—funded in part with moneys that Nader won in a suit against General Motors for following him with private detectives and attempting to entrap him with prostitutes—focused also on issues of road safety, although its major concerns were auto safety and product liability. The staff gave me great freedom and told me to read up in their small library, where I first encountered the "if you build it, they will come" phenomenon in road building and began to think about traffic calming before its time. As I recall, one of them directed me to a box of letters and documents that a Ford engineer with a conscience had given the Center. In the boxes I found discussion, in great detail, of the fact that the now infamous Ford "Pinto" was a fire hazard, that Ford knew about it and could have retrofitted the gas tanks on the vehicle for about $10 each, but insisted the Pinto was safe. The tank was visible under the rear bumper and held in place with two metal straps. In a rear-end collision, the tank might break loose, rupture, and spill gasoline; the horrible conflagrations led to dozens of deaths and disfiguring injuries. The Center offered "product liability" packages to trial lawyers to sue Ford on behalf of their clients, in this way forcing Ford and other automobile manufactures to pay greater attention to crashworthiness of their vehicles and no longer to shift the burden of responsibility for accidents entirely to suffering driver and passengers.

To many observers, it was not enough "to get drivers and pedestrians to behave appropriately." Evidence had accumulated by the 1960s that automobiles and roads could and must be made safer in the name of the public good. After a series of 1965 and 1966 Senate hearings, and with the support of the administration of President Lyndon Johnson, Congress voted unanimously to approve the Highway Safety Act and the National Traffic and Motor Vehicle Safety Act in 1966. It established the National Highway Safety Board (NHSB) known today as the National Highway Traffic Safety Administration (NHTSA), an organization intended to create regulations for vehicles and roads designed to be crashworthy.[1] The Johnson administration ordered the new

Department of Transportation to issue safety standards. It made manual seat belts compulsory in all cars beginning with 1968 models. In 1969 the government proposed requiring auto manufacturers to install air bags or passive restraints beginning with 1974 models; this was delayed several times over the years as manufacturers used the courts, lobbying, and administration change to postpone the regulation. But in 1977 the Carter Administration ordered all new full-size cars to have air bags or automatic restraints by 1982, and all cars by 1984.[2]

Safety engineers had long recognized the need to minimize impact intrusion into the passenger compartment, keep passengers within the vehicle during an accident with active and passive restraints, minimize the damage from deceleration and from sharp, hard surfaces, projectiles, and so on. Many of them knew Straith's work and all of them knew cadaver research, crash test dummies, and accident data. Over time, to protect occupants in automobiles, the engineers developed side guard door beams (metal beams inside doors to absorb crashes from the side), child safety locks, safety glass, anchored, ergonomic chairs, collapsing steering columns, padded dashboards, fire walls, crashworthy gas tanks, break-off mirrors, ABS (antilock breaking system, now mostly standard), and improved lighting.[3] Some of these improvements came in response to the National Motor Vehicle Traffic Safety Act; indeed in 1968 the NHTSA called for twenty-three improvements; manufacturers insisted that they—the technological pioneers of automobile luxury, power, and symbolic sexual prowess—impotently could manage only eighteen of them.[4] Manufacturers consistently argued that safety requirements would handicap their competitiveness with foreign manufactures and that the improvements were too costly, suggesting that they lacked the innovative verve that had at one time characterized the American industry.

Yet by the 1970s the idea of "crashworthiness"—the idea that automobile passengers should be protected in the event of a crash—had gained currency. Manufacturers, engineers, and government officials proposed both passive and active restraints; Jameson Wetmore notes they talked about "different ways of distributing responsibilities between automobile occupants, automobile manufacturers, and, to a lesser extent, government agencies." If at one time safety philosophy reflected the belief that the avoidance of collisions was the goal of safety, now they sought "engineering roads to limit the possibility of collisions and equipping vehicles with reliable brakes and steering; educating drivers and pedestrians on how to avoid collisions; and developing and enforcing rules of the road to compel drivers to carry out their responsibilities."[5]

Seat belts were first used on a 1949 Nash. Volvo patented the three-point seat belt in 1959 and made it available free of charge to all other manufacturers. The state of Victoria, Australia, first made seat belt use mandatory in 1970. But in many places, including in the United States, seat belts failed to work because people must consciously use them—and it took until the 1990s to pass laws in every state except NH to require their use. Sometimes people were lazy; other times they rejected the paternalistic attitude of the government for telling them they must use belts as infringement on personal liberty. In England a 1977 effort to make belts mandatory failed in the House of Lords after an emotional debate about acceptability of belts, enforcement problems, and issues of compulsion versus personal freedom.[6] Was liberty more important than life? In fact, a given severity of injury requires an average speed of 19 kilometers per hour greater speed to produce a similar injury if the occupant is belted. Being trapped in a burning car rarely happens, and thus the seat belt is the best choice. In nations such as Sweden that have long required mandatory seat belt use, the results—lower fatality and injury rates—have been clear.[7]

To avoid other technological approaches and implied liabilities, manufacturers worked to get states to pass laws requiring seat belt use and police to enforce these laws. One of the first technological efforts involved interlock devices and later passive restraints. I remember the passive system in my '89 Honda Accord. When you turned the ignition, the belt, affixed over the lap to a front shoulder belt carrier on the side window, would ride up and around the window frame to mimic a person pulling a three-point belt tight. Twice, when my visor was pulled to the side, the belt mechanism broke the visor off at its plastic anchor; it cost $59 to replace. The second time I insisted that Honda pay, which they did, and the third time I located a visor with a metal anchor at a junkyard.

US manufacturers, who had faced increasing losses in product liability cases, in particular with the Pinto, sought to avoid new safety requirements that they believed would hold them responsible for liability at higher standards. Automobile drivers and passengers meanwhile did not like irritating belts and restraints and whistles and bells; one presumes they did not like disfigurement or death, either. As a result, auto safety, like traffic calming, turned out to be a series of proposals, counterproposals, and debates about efficacy and safety that stalled practical and simple safety improvements.[8]

16 SAFETY DELAYS IN THE NAME OF FREEDOM

When Mercedes-Benz introduced airbags on some vehicles in the early 1980s and sought to bring them to the United States, they insisted these were a "supplemental restraint system" to work *with* the safety belts, not instead of, so that occupants still had responsibility to "buckle up." US manufacturers, too, bought into this approach because it put responsibility on occupants.

It was quite a battle to make airbags standard in US vehicles because of their untested nature, cost, and political opposition from antiregulatory individuals and business interests. In 1970 the director of the NHTSA issued a regulation requiring air bags in all passenger cars by July 1, 1973. The major automobile manufacturers took the NHTSA to court to argue that the technology was not feasible—and the courts agreed. In 1974 NHTSA announced such specifications, but the manufacturers again resisted and lobbied the Ford administration to delay further, even though Ford's transportation secretary, William Coleman, estimated that airbags would save 9,000 to 12,000 lives and untold numbers of injuries annually. Manufacturers worried that airbags would add $500 to the cost of a new car and passive seat belts about $100 per automobile.

Carter administration Secretary of Transportation Brock Adams promulgated a regulation that required passive restraints (either airbags or automatic shoulder belts) by 1981, while in 1977 the NHTSA issued a standard to require new cars to provide passive protection (airbags) to front occupants in severe crashes. The agency estimated this would save approximately 12,000 lives and prevent 104,000 serious injuries per year, while passive belts, if usage rates rose to 60 percent, would save 9,800 lives and prevent 117,000 injuries.[1] But before the standard took effect, Reagan's NHTSA administrator Raymond Peck determined to reject Adams's regulation because it would allow the automobile manufacturers to comply by furnishing a detachable form of passive restraint—shoulder belts—and to reject airbags, and since passengers would detach the device, nothing would be gained and it would be costly.[2] The insurance industry challenged the action in court for obvious reasons: more injuries and fatalities were costly to it. Ultimately the Washington, DC, Circuit Court overturned the NHTSA decision when it ruled that the NHTSA had an affirmative mandate to impose technology-forcing standards at the earliest possible date.[3]

But there were other reasons for safety delays under President Reagan. First, under his direction the federal government eased back on a wide range of auto-related regulations. While not the knee-jerk de-regulator that many of his nostalgic supporters proclaim him to be, he created an environment that encouraged the ascendency of antigovernment attitudes in general, and these slowed traffic calming. Upon becoming president, Reagan, former Hollywood actor and FBI informant, gutted Corporate Average Fuel Economy (CAFE) engine gas mileage standards, weakened bumpers,[4] and delayed or quashed many other rules. Crucially, he postponed mandatory airbags on all new automobiles into the 1990s with the result of how many deaths? Yet manufacturers now tout airbags as a selling point.[5]

The decision of the NHTSA under Reagan to back away from passive restraints and airbags led to a series of legal maneuvers to overturn that decision, and reveals in sharp relief how difficult it has been to use technologies—whether expensive like airbags, or simple like speed bumps—to make automobile travel safer. In this case, the delay was crucial since premature deaths among some age groups owing to car accidents exceeded those of a number of diseases and to economic costs of injuries of $24–$30 billion annually by the early 1980s. The NHTSA faced the problem that a declining number of people used seat belts. Rather than attempt to change behavior, the NHTSA turned to technological solutions such as seat belts that closed automatically when the door closed and air bags, both of which were effective and practicable.

17 SPEED BUMP DOWNSIDES

Opposition to speed bumps and other traffic-calming approaches mirrored that against air bags. It has been persistent, but opponents overlook or dismiss the point that safety and public health should come first, and the machine—the automobile—should be a final consideration. Opponents of speed bumps note that they can damage the suspension and front-end alignment of crossing vehicles and lead to loss of control for drivers of mopeds, motorcycles, and bicycles. Speed bumps slow the response time of emergency vehicles or cause loose objects to be thrown around in an ambulance, fire truck, or other vehicle. Many residents dislike them for their noise and claim that they lower property values. Some drivers "peel out" after crossing them in frustration. They cause a slight increase in gasoline consumption and emissions when drivers slow and accelerate. They can divert traffic to other roads so that the traffic becomes someone else's problem. Some critics even assert that speed bumps are dangerous because they lull the pedestrian into inattention and thus will assume that speed bumps and zebra crosswalks will slow vehicles without fail—and then will cease to look both ways.[1] But *any* pedestrian who forgets to look both ways hopes that the vehicle coming toward him is slowing or will stop if need be. This is hardly an argument to remove speed bumps.

Do speed bumps increase pollution? The question of the impact of traffic calming on fuel economy has been studied closely. According to one study, based on GPS data in conjunction with microscopic vehicle fuel consumption and emission models to quantify the energy and environmental impacts, speed bumps generated increases in vehicle fuel consumption up to 53 percent and significant increases in HC, CO, NO, and CO_2 emissions. The authors suggest instead using the traffic circle as the most effective traffic-calming approach in terms of energy and air quality savings.[2] But these increases in emissions occur briefly and only at the point of the calming technology, not for an entire trip, and calmed traffic is far less polluting than gridlocked traffic. Yet drivers sit in traffic for hours every day and do not complain about their low fuel consumption as they stop and start on their way to work. In fact, traffic calming has been surprisingly cost-effective. Discouraging traffic means no need to expand infrastructure for automobiles. Narrowing roads for sidewalks and bike paths means fewer repairs. Traffic calming leads to segregation of traffic and lower emissions, noise, and dangers so that public health improves.[3]

To deal with this issue, a number of countries have experimented with the speed hump or speed table to replace the speed bump. Humps trigger gradual slowing and acceleration. The speed hump and speed table rise to 7.5–8.0 centimeters over the roadway and continue for several meters, while the speed bump has an abrupt and higher rise and is mostly used in parking lots and shopping centers to this day.[4] Significant study has enabled optimal speeds to be matched with safety issues, potential damage to automobile suspension, and load-bearing questions. The speed bump—as cheaper and rudimentary—remains overwhelmingly the calming technology of choice outside of Europe and North America.

18 WAXING AND WANING OF BRAZILIAN SPEED BUMPS

Speed bumps have entered the pantheon of *Verkehrsberuhigung*, along with zebra crossings, traffic circles, and traffic signals in rural regions as well, and in countries undergoing rapid cultural and social change owing to industrialization, migration, and automobility. These pressures can be seen in cities, small towns, and in extensive rural spaces that seem to be empty but have indigenous people, local fishermen and craftsmen, farmers and peasants—for example in Siberia and the Russian Far North, and in Brazil in Amazonia. Brazil, a country of brilliant contrasts between urban and rural, built environments and rainforest, magnificent rivers and plantations of GMO soy, peasants and scientists, bureaucrats and gangs, 200,000 indigenes remaining from 5 million at first contact with the

Portuguese, and an innovator in genomics and aerospace, yet with a lawless agriculture of squatting, expropriation of land, uncertain titles, clear-cutting, and slash-and-burn, must in all of these spaces with all of these people struggle to reign in the automobile and the truck. Automobile fatality and injury rates have skyrocketed. Crosswalks, radar, photo-censors, and speed bumps (*lombada*) are the first salvo in the battle against the machine.

An international effort—the Decade of Action for Road Safety 2011–20—significantly reduced accident and fatality rates in many places. Europe succeeded in lowering traffic deaths by 17 percent since 2010, or roughly 9,000 people. In Brazil, rates are rising; over the last ten years, 41.7 percent more people died on Brazil's roads than on all of Europe's; in 2013 39,000 people perished in road accidents. The carnage in such poor states as Maranhão, Piauí, and Bahia is out of proportion to wealthier states,[1] suggesting yet again that speed bumps have class and gender. Pedestrians account for roughly 36 percent of all Brazilian road fatalities; this percentage is lower than in such developing countries as China, but significantly higher than in such developed countries as the United States. The danger to pedestrians in rural areas is greater, especially along two-lane roads.[2] Elderly people, motorcyclists, and rural residents are particularly vulnerable, as are those generally in the north and northeast regions with lower per capita GDP.[3] Might traffic-calming measures be brought to bear on these problems?

FIGURE 9 "Traffic Jam of Mopeds. Mapusa, Goa, India, 2014."
In many places, not even the moped and scooter are a solution
to traffic.
Courtesy of KatherineGo.

Brazil has a crude automobile mortality rate of 20.7
per 100,000 residents, in the top ten of the world. Brazil's
Ministry of Health wants to halve the number of deaths by
2020 through its *Vida no Trânsito* to introduce good driving
practices, and its Ministry of Cities called for traffic-calming
measures and safety improvements in urban transport.[4]
Education, fines, reduction of speeding, antialcoholism
campaigns, loss of licenses, and other restrictions have helped
somewhat, but more traffic calming—and speed bumps—
are needed.[5] The problem extends to Amazonia, even with
its low population densities, because of careless drivers and

miserable roads. Low-tech asphalt, rubber, and high-tech electronic speed bumps have thus entered the rainforest: along the Trans-Amazonian Highway they keep truckers alert and under risky speeds.

The 5,000 kilometer-long Trans-Amazonian highway runs from João Pessoa on the northeastern coast of Brazil to Peru. In the early 1970s the military leaders of Brazil pushed the highway through the rainforest as a technological solution to unemployment, hoping to attract settlers to interior regions of great natural resources and job potential, at the same time offering an alternative to the potential attraction of peasants to imagined communist insurgents. (The US Interstate Highway system was linked in name if not word with "defense" and the goal of securing the nation against Communist threats through commerce and mobility—including that of troops.) Rather than promote land reform and pry loose even modest parcels of land from the control of the wealthy landowning class, the Brazilian generals built a highway that attracted the rural poor to move further inland, but with few services or jobs. Like American officials and industrialists, they too assumed the road would automatically and autonomously bring goods, jobs, and prosperity. Perhaps they knew something of the US Homestead Acts, a series of laws dating to 1862 that enabled settlers a title to land of at least 160 acres. The US laws were intended to support a strong, independent, class of farmers, expand the economy, and secure land from Native Americans.

Brazilian leaders also expected the automobile to do its magic to facilitate the process of settlement. Former President Fernando Collor de Mello (1990–92), who raced cars for Puma Sports, saw the automobile as a savior for Brazil's economy. He forced the modernization of Brazil's automobile industry; it has grown to the tenth largest in the world. The government pursued tariffs and other controls to ensure this growth in competition with foreign manufacturers. Sixty-five percent of automobile content must be Brazilian and ten of twelve manufacturing steps must take place in Brazil, even if most Brazilian automobiles sport such names as Volkswagen, Ford, and Fiat.

The main highway and feeder roads of the Trans-Amazonian highway indeed attracted thousands of people, but the generals grew indifferent to the project, while successive governments have tried to repair, expand, and complete it in fits and starts. The road generally has brought state-sponsored environmental degradation and local frustrations. The mostly dirt highway becomes an impassible, muddy mess during rainy season. The road accelerated Amazonian deforestation and erosion by pushing logging, animal husbandry (beef), and slash-and-burn agriculture forward.

And there are speed bumps. The highway introduced high-speed dangers to Amazonia, especially on the outskirts of the towns that dot the vast territory. Truckers make money by delivering heavy loads as quickly as they can, and accident rates have grown with speed and distance. Truckers in many countries have the reputation of being scofflaws, or speeding, or driving beyond legal time-at-the-wheel limits. In the United States the trucking industry works tirelessly to free trucks from regulations it views as unnecessary, and with the assistance of Republicans in Congress trucking companies gained legislation to make trucks bigger, longer, and heavier, and to allow drivers to work longer hours with less rest, while prohibiting additional insurance requirements and removing some of the last legal speed bumps to public road safety regarding trucks.[6] The US death toll in truck-involved crashes rose 17 percent from 2009 to 2013. Fatalities in truck-involved crashes have risen four years in a row, reaching nearly 4,000 people in 2013, almost 600 of whom were truckers or their passengers. Large trucks are disproportionately involved in fatal accidents. According to the *New York Times*, "While heavy trucks accounted for less than 10 percent of total miles traveled in the United States during 2013, according to federal data, the NTSB [National Traffic Safety Board] recently reported that they were involved in one in eight of all fatal accidents and about one-quarter of all fatal accidents in work zones."[7] Yet Congress and the trucking industry want drivers to be younger, work longer hours, and escape new smart technologies that would make monitoring more systematic, let alone accident avoidance technology that would immediately enable higher safety standards. Why do these people want to roll back public safety? Are speed bumps an unnecessary government regulation?

Brazilian truckers are no different. They are forced to work long hours by profit-seeking companies, or if self-employed by breakneck competition and lack of regulation. They need to make up for lost time when they get stuck in mud, so they speed whenever they can, and pedestrians suffer for it. According to the World Health Organization, "Road traffic crashes [in Brazil] are a leading cause of death, injury and hospitalization, resulting in high economic and social costs."[8] Speed bumps and traffic calming have thus become necessary not only in Brazil's urban centers, but in rural regions.

Between Marabá and Pacaja the BR 163 carries impatient truckers through its twists and turns, although during rainy season they often have to wait for a front-end loader to tow them from waist-deep mud. The government is contracting with private companies to "embark on a $417 million paving project to turn BR163 into a modern two-lane toll highway" to link soy culture and Amazon River ports. The trucks fly along highways, and to provide some margin of safety there will be an occasional speed bump.[9] As they do everywhere, because speed is their wage earner, the drivers criticize speed bumps for damaging suspension and being square to their wheels.[10] They seem also not to slow down the trucks. In several cases, local residents have reacted furiously to accidents in which friends and family have died at the wheels of truckers; they shut down traffic and harangue police and officials. In June 2015 along the BR 230 in Sousa, Pariaba, they set up a flaming speed bump of tires, logs, and branches to protest a fatal accident that killed one person and seriously injured another.[11]

In rural Mexico, too, speed bumps—*topes* or *bustos*—protect the entrances and exits of small towns. They come in concrete blocks, iron bullets, a series of them like a washboard called *vibradores* (vibrators),[12] and even burlap bags of carrots. Unlike speed bumps in the United States, Canada or Europe the Mexican *bustos* "inspire fear," sneaking up on the driver and lacking warning signs and paint. After assaulting the undercarriage, muffler, axle, and oil pan, they launch the driver into the air. One journalist concluded, "They are, in a word, diabolical."[13]

Like traffic planners in other countries, Brazilian specialists have determined in essence to rely on drivers to make smart choices rather than to inconvenience them and their vehicles. This country of Embraeier Jets and GMOs (genetically modified organisms) has turned to "electronic speed bumps"—in fact cameras that take photographs of speeding drivers and cars. The National Department of Infrastructure and Transport is responsible for installation of radars and electronic signaling.[14] In true high-tech form, the government developed the "Spine," the Electronic Speed Reducer, which employs image-capture data-processing software to regulate speed and flow at such critical points as dangerous curves and locations with poor visibility and where there are many pedestrians, even in the rainforest.[15] These radars can operate at all hours of the day to ensure constant speeds, lower them at peak times, and be turned off at night. (Don't people speed at night?) Drivers who exceed the speed limit are fined according to an ascending speed scale and get points on their licenses. The installation of the spines and speed bumps along the BR230 in 2011 led to a decline in severity and number of accidents by nearly 50 percent, the number of injured by nearly 55 percent, and deaths by 25 percent.[16]

19 POTHOLES AND PAPER MONEY

Ти моя остання любов,

Моя машина, моя машина.

Ти і я напилися знов,

Моя єдина

На смак бензина—кави.

День і ніч дихає час, А ми з тобою живемо двоє.

Автомобіль буде у нас, Моє ти сонце.[1]

—OKEAN ELZY

When the Berlin Wall crumbled in 1989, Hungary was one of the first countries to open borders fully with Western Europe through Austria, with Vienna only three hours by train from Budapest. (Hungary's right-wing government in 2015 has sought to close borders to immigrants, and in general has picked away at citizens' rights, leaving them only with their automobiles.) East Germans could not wait to get to West Berlin. En masse they drove to Hungary, parked their "Trabbies" (the DDR's indestructible, highly polluting people's automobile, the *Trabant*) helter-skelter on the streets, left the keys in the ignition, and hopped the train to Vienna to get to West Germany. Hungarians assumed ownership of the Trabbies, and also began buying new and used cars from abroad, flooding their towns and cities with vehicles, overwhelming road infrastructure, generating traffic jams of epic proportions, and filling the air with noxious fumes, the streets with petrochemical sheen, and the Danube with multicolored oil slicks. But these problems—traffic, pollution, noise, costly road repairs and construction— were unimportant to many citizens in the first postsocialist years, because the automobile was a symbol of freedom, of consumer culture, of a society where individuals had the right to go where they wanted when they wanted. The fight against traffic speed, crowding, and pollution through speed bumps and zebra crosswalks has been grudging.

It's worse in Russia. Everyone wants an automobile and sees it as a symbol of freedom. Muscovites willingly tolerate legendary traffic jams that begin at 7:00 a.m. and end at 8:00 p.m. for that vestige of freedom. Moscow is privileged to have President Putin in the Kremlin. This means the city commands a disproportionate share of resources and power, and attracts a disproportionate share of automobiles and road projects. Moscow grows, while sixty-six of Russia's eight-three regions have lost population since the last census.

Moscow has the world's greatest subway system. It was built with gulag prisoners, many of whom perished with picks in their hands, and opened in 1935 with one line, 11 kilometers in length. Its grandiose thirteen stations of marble and steel anointed in socialist realist style celebrated the worker and the state. Stalin argued that the capitalist worker suffered through long monotonous daily commutes and toiled in dark and din, while the socialist metro ensured the worker arrived at work and at home invigorated and refreshed. By 2016 the Moscow metro had tunneled to over 200 stations and 329 kilometers in total length, with over thirty stations (under construction) and another fifty more stations forecast. It's magnificent, and it moves traffic! Yet Muscovites prefer to sit in gridlock and arrive at work exhausted and angry. Moscow's 11.5 million residents, with an estimated 3 million more unregistered residents, and hundreds of thousands of daily passers-through seeking business, goods, and services, have at least 4.5 million vehicles, or one in ten of all automobiles in Russia. The automobile is the major source of pollution in Russia by far, and much of that pollution is in Moscow.

Russia's political system has become closed to participation and dissent, NGOs are under attack, foreigners have fallen under suspicion, and President Putin's political party, Russia United, rules unencumbered by opposition. As a result of economic policy based solely on resource extraction for the benefit of oligarchs and their male friends, the plummeting of oil and gas prices, and sanctions because of Russia's war on Ukraine and annexation of Crimea, recession has set in, the budget has tightened, the military takes a larger share, and social programs, education, and other important government activities have suffered immensely—but what worries many Russians is how bad the roads are and how poorly their government maintains them or builds new infrastructure to handle the growing number of vehicles. They want potholes repaired, not traffic calmed through speed bumps—or sleeping policemen as they are called. Yet road building may be the most corrupt area of the economy. And so Russians hold on to their freedom while sitting in traffic; many refuse to use seat belts, considering them infringement on their rights. And tens of thousands die annually in crashes that have their place in YouTube lore under the rubric "We Love Russia."

Russian drivers have a unique sense of safety and propriety. In the provinces they often occupy the oncoming traffic lane on two-lane roads, certain that it is in better shape than their proper lane. On the return trip, they again occupy the oncoming traffic lane, certain that it, too, is in better shape than the proper lane. And no one yields right-of-way. A friend, the vice mayor of Severodvinsk, once drove me to a friend's summer home. We came to a traffic light, second in line. By the time the light changed to green, roughly fifteen other drivers had surrounded us, each trying to be the first into the intersection. I asked, "Who has the right-of-way?" He answered "Everyone."

As Stan Lugar reminds us, while familiar to us and embedded in daily life, the automobile is unnatural. It requires us to rebuild nature to meet its own needs, not necessarily those of citizens. It is "a blend of modern technology and individualism." It merges "power and violence, freedom and sexuality." Advertisements—and our thoughts—equate the car with success. Yet in its influence on family life, dating patterns, suburban development, air and noise pollution, and fatality rates, it overwhelms our social and political institutions. Lugar writes, "The endless highways of our metropolitan landscapes, often choked with traffic, evoke many of the contradictions of modern society. While individual cars offer convenience and mobility, they become increasingly less practical with each additional care they have to compete with."[2] These notions hold for Russia as much as they do for the United States, the Netherlands, Brazil, and elsewhere. The question is when, if at all, and in what ways, citizens can reign in the power of the automobile to influence our choices in other realms of life—for example, through traffic calming.

The enigmatic automobile suggested that even in classless Soviet society the automobile indicated class and status. A possession of wealthy Communist Party officials, often with chauffeurs—or perhaps the proud purchase of the dedicated worker, or even the lucky stash of another citizen, mostly likely a male—they became required possessions of Russians after the breakup of the USSR, a sign of freedom, independence, and the epitome of consumer culture.[3] The Soviet industry produced two million vehicles in 1987 and then collapsed as the economy spun down into deep depression. At first most consumers could afford to buy only used vehicles, a large share of which came from Europe; in Siberia and the Far East Japanese (right-side driver) vehicles tended to dominate. In the western regions consumers coveted BMWs and Mercedes. But most of those vehicles were old used cars that brought significant repair, pollution, and safety problems eastward into Russia.

Even in the economic and political crises of the 1990s, car ownership—and road lawlessness—grew rapidly. From 1995 to 2006, private car ownership grew almost twofold, as the Russian industry recovered and foreign companies invested heavily in Russian production. Many analysts expected Russia's oil economy and consumer demand to make it Europe's largest car market by 2015. Yet the decline in oil prices, and the sanctions on the Russian economy because of its annexation of Crimea and war in Ukraine, have led to recession in which both Russian and foreign manufacturers have pulled back significantly. GM closed its plant near St. Petersburg, Russia, in March 2015, wrote off hundreds of millions of dollars in investment, and ended its joint venture with GAZ (the Gorky Automobile Factory) to produce Chevrolets, as the market dropped suddenly by 50, 60, even 80 percent.[4]

Infrastructure has not kept up with the needs of drivers, and most new construction takes place near centers of power—Moscow and St. Petersburg—while road construction lags significantly throughout the rest of the vast nation. Traffic jams and miserable roads cripple Ekaterinburg, the fourth largest city in Russia, while a promised new subway line may never be finished. Drivers have taken over lanes dedicated to trams and the police are powerless to prevent them. Everywhere road crews struggle to fill potholes, let alone keep roads open. *Gastarbeiter*, from the Central Asian nations who used to be part of the USSR, provide most of the labor from Moscow to the Ural Mountains to Tomsk to Vladivostok and are excellent workers, yet they struggle with racist bosses, unsafe conditions, and outdated machinery that at best adheres thin strips of asphalt on poorly prepared roadbed. As a result, the quality of the roads lags considerably, by international—and Russian—standards. Might permafrost serve as a speed bump?

Excessive accident, fatality, and injury rates have accompanied the rise of automobile culture. The average automobile fatality rate in the world is 18 per 100,000 fatalities, down from 20.8 in 2000, highest in the African region (24.1 per 100,000), and lowest in the European region (10.3 per 100,000). Russia, at 18.6, has a 50 percent higher fatality rate than the United States (11.6), a bit less than Brazil (22.5), and five times the rate in Netherlands (3.9). The authorities claim that poor roads are the single most important factor in fatalities, leading to a quarter of the dead and injured, with maintenance, signage, and other problems—particularly at pedestrian crossings that Russian drivers relish to ignore—following just behind. Drunk driving caused about 2,100 deaths of 35,000 fatalities in 2013. Young males are particularly at risk of dying from road traffic crashes. Another danger is the "capsule of death." Today's virtually unregulated minivan buses in Russian cities, used by students, working poor, and pensioners, along with such tin cans as the tiny Daewoo "Matiz," are called "capsules of death" for their frequency of accidents and poor crashworthiness with risk to passengers, drivers, and pedestrians alike. Russia, per capita, per kilometer traveled or by any other metric, is a dangerous place in need of speed bumps.[5]

The Russian Federation has achieved a slight improvement in safety performance. Between 2004 and 2008, even with a 24 percent increase in traffic volume, there was a 13 percent reduction in deaths. This downward trend has continued. Over the first seven months of 2014, the number of speed-related road accidents dropped by 61.9 percent, with fatalities falling by 59.9 percent and injuries by 60.8 percent.[6] However, the road safety situation continues to be serious and challenging. In a recent year, the estimated socio-economic cost of road crashes was over RUR 908 billion (around US $29 billion), representing over 2 percent of GDP. When compared internationally (and taking into account differences in definitions of fatality), death rates in crashes on Russian roads are five times as high as experienced in the global best-performing nations in road safety.[7]

My experience is that Russian drivers consider the pedestrian a "sport," and hence the decline in pedestrian fatalities indicates that perhaps drivers have developed new, progressive cultural norms. In other ways, though, there is a long, pothole-filled road to traverse. Specialists studying the Lipetsk region determined than only 55 percent of drivers used seat belts; 58 percent of front seat passengers but only 9 percent of back seat passengers, and shockingly only 11 percent of cars with children, had any type of child safety measure. In the United States, 87 percent of drivers use belts and the percent has been rising for over a decade.[8] On urban roads Russian drivers were less likely to wear seat belts compared to those on main highways and rural roads, even though most people seem to understand that "seat belts save lives."[9] This is a culture of feigned attention to safety practices and ingrained road rage, as myriad video clips on the internet will confirm.

If one accepted a geographically determinist explanation of history, then the presence of unsafe roads in Russia devolves directly from weather and climate, and we can also blame invasions of the Varangians (eighth century), Mongols (thirteenth century), and Swedes (sixteenth century) for their wars on Russian infrastructure. But Canada, Norway, Sweden, and Finland could equally make the same arguments about geography and weather, low population densities, and other factors; they recognize the challenges of making their roads safe, both in the cities and provinces, yet manage to do so in all weather. Russian roads, on the other hand, suffer not only from poor driving culture, but also from inattention, corruption, and poor building practices that exacerbate the weather problems, while traffic-calming culture remains in its infancy.

If President Putin is determined to modernize Russia, shouldn't communication infrastructure be at the top of the list—rather than oil and gas fields? In the destitute 1990s the country built about 6,000 kilometers of roads annually. Under Putin the number dropped to about 2,000–3,000 kilometers annually. The World Economic Forum places Russian roads in 125th place of 139 ranked nations. Poor roads increase transit costs; *Rosavtodor* (the Federal Road Agency of the Ministry of Transportation, an organization with Tsarist roots whose problems remain those of the Tsarist era—miserable roads, railroads, and other communications services in the countryside) estimates direct losses for insufficient development of roads at hundreds of billion rubles annually.

Lawlessness on Russian roads is one thing that Russians can count on, and it begins with corruption in their construction. Russians are aware of the "inexplicable mystery" of the high cost of road construction that is several times higher than in other countries—even if the road industry employs relatively cheap Kazakh, Kirgiz, Uzbek, and Tadjik laborers. The Russians spend more for roads and get less than anyone else.[10] In the first half of 2015 alone in Ulianovsk, prosecutors uncovered corruption in a contract worth over 100 million rubles.[11] In Stavropol'e— "the roads lead to hell" according to local reports—over 400 million rubles were wasted on roads, bridges, and safety improvements in terms of tempo and quality of work. This led to the firing of one construction company, the replacement by another, and such practices as using concrete blocks rather than poured concrete and laying earth rather than sand and gravel as foundation, as the accompanying paperwork had been doctored to indicate.[12]

The 2015 Russian federal budget for road construction and repairs was nearly 70 billion rubles—approximately $100 million—something on the order of the entire budget of the state of Maine, and with very little for speed bumps and other traffic-calming measures. According to the general director of the Institute of Regional Problems, Dmitri Zhuravlev, these funds permit improvements for roughly 3,500 kilometers of roadway, but the regional network of roads in Russia is over 500,000 kilometers in total, many of them are dirt and gravel, and because of endemic corruption this leaves them unfinished, poorly finished, or below technical standards.[13]

The danger of endemic corruption may well play out in a proposed 5-kilometer-long bridge from across the Sea of Azov to Crimea that Russia annexed from Ukraine in March 2014 at the close of the Sochi Winter Games. The bridge, with another 14 kilometers of approaches and ramps, will have parallel road and railroad sections. It is a symbol of Russian control of the region, its imperial aspirations, and the close contacts between President Vladimir Putin and wealthy oligarchs who dominate Russian resources of oil, gas, timber, nickel, platinum, and the nuclear and construction industries. In this case Putin's friend and judo partner, Arkadii Rotenberg, head of the massive construction and energy firm, Stroigazmontaszh, has promised to build the bridge at a cost of 230 billion rubles ($4 billion) by 2018. Rotenberg was thrilled to undertake this project as his "final big project and not for the purpose of making money. It is, if you will, my contribution to the development of the country." Ignoring Russia's military aggression, he continued, "The need for construction of a bridge across the Kerch Strait existed in Soviet times, but after the Crimean peninsula returned to Russia."[14] Who returned it? And did they encounter any bumps on the way?

Rotenberg has claimed that he will not exceed the $4 billion allotted, although cost overruns for Russia are as regular as heavy snows in Tomsk. (I estimate $8 billion when finished and 2020 as the year of completion.) The budget for the Sochi games, which involved Stroigazmontazh among other oligarchic contractors, came in at an obscene $53 billion and caused massive environmental degradation.[15] The Kerch Bridge will serve wealthy BWM and Mercedes owners trying to get to Crimean resorts without passing through the Ukrainian war zone. Engineering surveys, bridge design, blueprints, and other works have been completed, and, no doubt just as in Sochi, the authorities assure us that the budget includes significant archaeological research and environmental activities.[16] Above all else, the Kerch Bridge is an enabler of automobiles. It has a design capacity of 40,000 automobiles and forty-seven locomotive trains along two tracks per day. Unfortunately, most of the other roads in the area have not been repaired in ten years and with funds going to the bridge, what will be left over? And, will there be any money left for speed bumps in Crimea in the face of the onslaught of automobiles from Kerch?

Indeed, it's the Russian tradition to fund big projects with great ideological significance that are finished poorly and with delay, and to ignore the small folk and their needs, so why would the Kerch Bridge be different? Peter the Great's St. Petersburg, built by conscripted peasants who gathered mud from the Neva River Delta in their shirts and perished in the summer swamps and winter cold; Stalin's White Sea-Baltic Canal and Magnitogorsk, a mismanaged, highly polluting steel city in the Urals; the Kuibyshev Hydroelectric Power Station of the 1950s, built with 200,000 gulag prisoners; Leonid Brezhnev's new Trans-Siberian railroad, BAM, declared a "project of the century" when officially completed in 1981, but in fact ill-completed only twenty years later: but nary a speed bump. As Latour tells us, the speed bump is not a lump of asphalt.

FIGURE 10 Francisco Anzola, "Moscow Traffic." WikiCommons, October 2, 2007.

Russia cannot fill potholes, let alone consider curb cuts or build speed bumps.[17] The situation is so bad that the authorities created an interactive map where citizens may register and then specify locations of problems.[18] Instead, much of the money intended to fix potholes flows into pothole construction firms' pockets. In Apatity, in Murmansk Province—a vast Arctic region with unusually good roads for Russia owing to permafrost, ledge, and the absence of mud and swamp—the authorities have taken to painting potholes rather than filling them to encourage drivers, one supposes, to zigzag to avoid them. This was necessary because in brutally cold weather and the need for the material to set right, asphalt-manufacturing facilities would not be operating until mid-June.[19] In Petropavlovsk-Kamchatka, the authorities repaired potholes with plywood and nails that lasted less than an hour.[20] In the city of Arsen'ev, having failed to get the authorities to do anything about potholes, a "flashmob" of drivers calling themselves Arskontrol DPS poured thousands of coins and even bills into a hole then put a thin layer of concrete on top, to make the point that "it is more effective to fill road hazards with money than to pay transportation taxes and see no results."[21] Arskontrol, at least, was a good name. Or, as Russians often say, "Vodka without beer is like throwing money into the wind."

Hence persistent political, legal, psychological, and climatological challenges prevent a systematic approach to traffic calming in Russia; the physical problems center on the design and layout of Russian towns and cities. Massive thoroughfares designed in the Soviet era, perhaps to permit rapid movement of military vehicles, are in essence difficult to calm because of the volume of traffic and the challenges to erecting barriers and speed bumps, or narrowing roads. No neighborhoods are amenable to the *woonerf* approach; car owners park wherever they wish, in courtyards, on sidewalks, and expect pedestrians to get out of the way. Pedestrian malls face not only the cost of creating physical space, but also fear among officials that they might serve as a gathering place for dissidents. The police have resorted to cardboard police officers holding radar guns to slow drivers. Nothing works. Russian drivers hate and ignore rumble strips, too, while the federal and municipal road services see no future in sleeping policeman.

Indeed as of 2008, according to the GOST (State Standard) R52605-2006, drivers can sue the authorities for damage to their automobiles because of improperly installed speed bumps. GOST R 52605-2006 for "Artificial Surface Irregularity" updated GOST N184-F3 (December 27, 2002), and it sought to standardize approaches to safety improvements on the nation's roads. According to the standards, speed bumps were intended to reduce speed to less than 40 kilometers/hour, especially near schools, playgrounds, places of public entertainment, at dangerous, unregulated intersections with unsecured visibility of vehicles, and other such places. The Russian law limits installation of speed bumps to road sections with artificial lighting. They may not be installed on federal highways, roads with four or more lanes, on bridges, underpasses or in tunnels.

Several online Web pages, including official ones, offered advice for drivers on how to approach "sleeping policemen" as they proliferated not only on roads near schools and playgrounds, but at such dangerous areas as curves and especially in store parking lots. Using "physics," one Web page noted that a major mistake of drivers was to approach the speed bump with a foot on the brake, which could lead to damage to the front suspension; the proper way was to brake beforehand and to accelerate when the front wheels passed over the bump. The police actually advised that if a driver saw a sleeping policeman too late, "Do not brake, but perhaps even add a little gas."[22] There are many speed bumps throughout the nation of different size and shape so that, "even at a speed of 40 km a vehicle with small clearance . . . can be damaged."[23] One site, "Eliminate Automobile Illiteracy (*Avtolikbez*)," run by a journalist and actor who loves automobiles and automobile races, entertained a forum about speed bumps with one reader claiming that "they wanted the best, but it turned out as always": they imported speed bumps from the "cursed West," forgetting that the West has law-abiding drivers.[24]

And what of sleeping policemen? The authorities have begun a journey into modernity and traffic control, but progress is slow. Over the summer of 2014 Ekaterinburg traffic officials modestly installed four sets of traffic lights and sixteen speed bumps and painted fifteen new pedestrian crossings with zebra-yellow bright paint. Five other speed bumps were planned before the school year began in ten days, according to the deputy mayor.[25] Nationwide, newspapers dutifully cover the installation of each new speed bump: "From the Photograph Evidence, It's Clear: In Syktyvkar [in the Komi Republic] Another 'Sleeping Policeman' Appeared"[26]; in Omsk, another thirty-seven of them, mostly near to schools and kindergartens[27]; in Vologda, a city of 300,000 northeast of Moscow, the traffic department removed four speed bumps because of lower accident rates, but will monitor the situation and re-install them if accidents so indicate. In 2015 there were forty-two speed bumps in all in Vologda, and the department plan to replace them but are waiting for proposals from drivers themselves about other schema for calming.[28] In Perm, in the northern foothills of the Ural Mountains, a city of one million people once known as Molotov after Stalin's right-hand man, and still known for its connection to the prison industry, fifty-five speed bumps were installed near schools in summer 2015.[29] Irkutsk administrators hoped that an integrated approach to traffic calming would add to safety of pedestrians in the city. In 2015 the administration planned to install seven new traffic lights, to repair four others, and to add speed bumps and guardrails at thirty pedestrian crossings, with another sixteen lights projected for 2016. They even talked about using footbridges over traffic instead, especially in center city where such a bridge might cost $1 million.[30]

Citizen-pedestrians apparently would like to see more speed bumps installed for their safety and that of their children. But they feel increasingly powerless to fight automobility and get speed bumps installed, since the 2008 national standards for the "sleeping policemen" went into effect. In Tver, the Department of Highway and Transportation maintains that, according to the standards, it cannot install any more speed bumps, although it will employ flashing yellow lights. Only at elementary and middle schools, playgrounds, places of public entertainment, stadiums, railway stations, shops, and "other facilities of the mass concentration of pedestrians" are sleeping policeman permitted, and not at any other location simply to control excessive speed.[31]

Moscow benefits from traffic calming involuntarily with the massive back up of traffic every day. Moscow is a black hole of resources and political power, yet is unable to transform itself from a parking lot into a great nation's capital city. Muscovites average a commute of 1.5 hours each way and a two-hour trip is not out of the ordinary; traffic takes 50 percent longer than it would with clear streets. If Moscow administrators claim they are dealing with the problem successfully, then drivers there, in St. Petersburg and other cities, know they are not, and even minor improvements in Moscow may be a mirage. Moscow established a Center for Organizing Road Movement that reduced traffic somewhat through "the elimination of chaotic parking." Only people with flashing blue lights, *migalki*, on top of their vehicles— officials and others who have bought influence—seem able to get through the snarled roads. A motorist rights group, the Blue Buckets, protest by taping blue buckets to the roofs of their cars.[32]

Thus, in spite of having the mightiest subway system in the world, Moscow's drivers would rather sit in gridlock in cars and listen to *Okean Elzy* or *Akvarium* or some other rock group, do their make-up, and occasionally engage in road rage. As for pedestrians, there may be hope—especially given the fact that a disproportionate share of the nation's road works is concentrated in Moscow. The city government has endorsed a plan for scores of raised pedestrian crossings—speed humps—at 10 centimeters versus 4 to 6 centimeters for speed bumps, and will also add a wide number of zebra crossings, especially in areas with a large number of accidents, close to schools and other educational institutions, metro stations, major shopping and business centers, cultural institutions, recreational areas, and tourist pedestrian routes.[33]

20 SPEED BUMPS FOR OTHER HOPEFUL TECHNOLOGIES

The editors of a special journal issue on road safety in global perspective recently observed that the motor vehicle is a contested technology, with adherents exhibiting "unhindered enthusiasm" and opponents showing "deeply entrenched opposition."[1] The speed bump is an attempt to moderate this contention, permitting automobiles to move to destinations without passing through residential areas at high speed, and giving some solace to those residents, their children, and their pets, as they walk and play safely unencumbered by noise, emissions, and filth. The speed bump represents the promise of traffic-calming measures. It is a symbol of hope that citizens, planners, and elected officials can take control of the built environment to ensure the presence of human scales and sensibilities. It serves humans while informing machines and their owners that they must come second in matters of health, safety, and aesthetics. The speed bump—together with signage, signals, laws, and fines; with road narrowing and curves; with sidewalks and dedicated bicycle lanes; with one-way streets, culs-de-sac, and other obstructions; with roundabouts; with entire neighborhoods designed to minimize automobility; and with efforts to make central in our lives quieter, more environmentally sound transportation technologies such as the bus, tram, and bicycle—can protect neighborhoods, homes and stores, churches, mosques and synagogues, athletic fields and parks from high-speed, high-volume, highly polluting traffic. In this way, the speed bump serves as a low-tech solution to a problem of high-tech origin. A simple mound of concrete or asphalt; a rubberized bump; a platform with a crosswalk on top: all of these things encourage the automobilist to think and perhaps even to slow down. The modern vehicle with its safety features, air conditioning, surround sound, Bluetooth, safety glass, and internal combustion engines can be made to follow, not lead, planning, and to slow, not accelerate, around children and cyclists. No amount of hurry justifies the risk of injury or death to oneself or others.

Why pay for self-drive automobiles to secure safety? The automobile is never a panacea. Why not use traffic calming to force the automobile off the residential street into the garage where it belongs and subsidize public transport so it is clean, fast, and safe? The automobile and highway are too expensive to maintain. What is the solution? Speed bump. The roads are full to capacity and commuting times are increasing. What is the solution? Speed bump.

Speed bump obstructions, whether horizontal or vertical, jog us awake from our complacency, apathy, and our inattention to others and the world around us. They remind us that people's lives are more important than an automobile's speed, and that policies dedicated to giving the automobile veto power over other plans for improvements in the built environment can be reversed or moderated, surprisingly, by those very obstructions. Sometimes there *is* a technological solution to a problem of technological origin. Growing population and affluence are the key drivers of anthropogenic stress on the environment. But these demographic and economic forces can in part be offset by politicians and citizens supportive of the environment. A recent study demonstrated that increases in emissions over time are lower in states that elect legislators with strong environmental records.[2] Or, as they say, you get what you pay for. And if speed bumps discourage private automobile use, then we have paid cheaply for better public health, a cleaner environment, and lower risk of accidents.

Speed bumps, in connection with other traffic-calming measures and re-funding of public transport, may have other significant social and public health benefits. Suburban "sprawl," for example, with its de rigueur automobile-based lifestyle, its direct and indirect interference with walking and exercise, may contribute to obesity, hypertension, diabetes, and coronary heart disease, although the relationships between sprawl, behavior, and weight are not fully clear.[3] But I have hope in the symbolism of the speed bump and in its concrete impact on behaviors—and on traffic, safety, and public health. It leads me to think about "speed bumps" for other seemingly self-augmenting and hard-to-control or regulate technologies. I lobbied for speed bumps to be installed on my college campus for over twelve years—they were finally installed when it became clear how dangerous automobile traffic on campus had become.

Many of the problems connected with traffic danger reflect "improvements" from a different era: higher traffic speed, increased access through wider roads and access thoroughfares, undifferentiated road systems, poor segregation of traffic categories, long straight streets, and a large number of parked cars in heavy traffic areas. These improvements for the automobile increased the risks of accidents, injuries, and fatalities for people in areas with many shops and schools, and they restricted space for playgrounds and parks. The segregation of traffic categories, culs-de-sac, loop streets, the *woonerf*, and the beloved speed bump was an attempt to make life to emphasize human aesthetics while simultaneously reducing these risks.

Communities—whether progressive or not—ultimately embrace speed bumps because speed bump technologies are local and democratic. They do not discriminate against any disadvantaged group, unless automobile drivers belong to a special group with special rights. They give all citizens positive feelings about their neighborhoods and a sense of ownership of the street. Residents are more likely to walk or bicycle, to value increased safety, enjoy improved air quality, experience reduced crime, and feel less dependence on personal modes of internal combustion transportation. Some people worry that, at first, pedestrians may have a false safety, overemphasizing the impact of speed bumps, perhaps crossing without the same careful attention to traffic that they would without bumps, failing to look both left and right, on top of which there is no one proven design standard as a panacea to calm traffic in every neighborhood. But we know that they are effective. Imagine a world with speed bumps for GMOs, guns, and vulgarity.

FIGURE 11 Putting up new traffic signal, San Diego, California, 1944. Perhaps there are ways to stop traffic.
Courtesy of Russell Lee, photographer, US Farm Security Administration, Office of War Information, in Library of Congress, fsa 8c00313 at //hdl.loc.gov/loc.pnp/fsa.8c00313.

NOTES

Introduction

1 Gareth Collingwood, "Dead Cops and Donkey Backs," March 3, 2013, http://elpedalero.com/?p=3465. If several in a row, *vibradores* (vibrators). *Despertador* (alarm clock, but a cross between a speed bump and a rumble strip).

2 http://www.alibaba.com/showroom/speed-hump.html

3 See "Traffic Calming Assessment," http://ddot.dc.gov/service/traffic-calming-assessment and "Speed Hump Request," http://ddot.dc.gov/node/545032, both as accessed June 16, 2015. See also "Traffic Calming 101," http://ddot.dc.gov/node/545512.

4 Asha Weinstein and Elizabeth Deakin, "A Survey of Traffic Calming Practices in the United States," University of California, Department of City and Regional Planning, ITE Annual Meeting, Monterey, California, March 1998.

5 Weinstein and Deakin, "A Survey."

6 Andrew Gorosko, "Queen Street Resident Urges More Speed Bumps," *Newtown (CT) Bee*, April 4, 2013, http://www.newtownbee.com/news/0001/11/30/queen-street-resident-urges-more-speed-bumps/13734. See also Dirk Pitt, "Remove

All Speed Bumps from Queen Street," https://www.change. org/p/the-police-commission-of-newtown-connecticut- remove-all-speed-bumps-from-queen-st, accessed October 3, 2015.

Chapter 1

1 Anna Kaltygina, "Spiashchie Politseiskie': Sprashivali, Otvechaem," August 23, 2012, http://auto.tut.by/news/ exclusive/306607.html.

2 "Lezhachie Politseiskie," 2014, http://www.tomovl.ru/ transportation/Lezhachiy_police.html, accessed July 10, 2015.

3 "V Kuressaare Poiavilis' Spiashchie Politseiskie," April 24, 2007, http://rus.delfi.ee/daily/criminal/v-kuressaare- poyavilis-spyaschie-policejskie?id=15649639, and "Spiashchie Politseiskie iz Aktobe Uvoleny za Narushenie Profetiki," September 9, 2014, http://www.24.kz/ru/novosti2/ proisshestvie/item/24768-v-aktobe-uvolili-politsejskikh- usnuvshikh-v-sluzhebnom-avtomobile.

4 Ivan Krishkevich, "'Lezhachikh Politseiskikh' Men'she ne Stanet, no ikh Dopolniat Drugie Sredstva Organizatsii Dorozhnogo Dvizheniia," *Avtoportal*, April 12, 2015, http:// www.abw.by/news/181790/.

5 "Stroitel'stvo 3-i Linii Minskogo Metro—Diuzhina Voprosov i Otvetov," *Minsk-Novosti*, July 31, 2014, http://minsknews. by/blog/2014/07/31/stroitelstvo-3-y-linii-minskogo-metro- dyuzhina-voprosov-i-otvetov/.

6 Congressional Budget Office, *Public Spending on Transportation and Water Infrastructure, 1956 to 2014* (Washington, DC: CBO, March 2015), pp. 8, 10, 12, 14.

7 Ingrid van Schagen, ed., *Traffic Calming Schemes: Opportunities and Implementation Strategies* (Leidschendam: SMOV Institute for Road Safety Research, 2003), R-2003-22, pp. 11–12.

8 Schagen, *Traffic Calming Schemes*, pp. 13–14.

9 Herman Huang and Michael Cynecki, *The Effects of Traffic Calming Measures on Pedestrian and Motorist Behavior* (McLean, VA: Federal Highway Administration, US Department of Transportation, 2001).

10 Schagen, *Traffic Calming Schemes*, p. 23.

11 C. D. Allen and L. B. Walsh, "A Bumpy Road Ahead," *Traffic Engineering*, October 1975, pp. 11–14.

12 Schagen, *Traffic Calming Schemes*, pp. 3–4.

Chapter 2

1 Mike Maciag, "Skyrocketing Court Fines Are Major Revenue Generator for Ferguson," August 22, 2014, http://www.governing.com/topics/public-justice-safety/gov-ferguson-missouri-court-fines-budget.html.

2 Bruno Latour, *Pandora's Hope: Essays on the Reality of Science Studies* (Cambridge: Harvard University Press, 1999), p. 190.

Chapter 3

1 Clark Willis, "Skycraper Utopias: Visionary Urbanism in the 1920s," in *Imagining Tomorrow*, ed. Joseph Corn (Cambridge:

MIT Press, 1986); Richard Stites, "Utopia in Space: City and Building" in his *Revolutionary Dreams: Utopian Vision and Experimental Life* (New York: Oxford University Press, 1981); and Howard Segal, *Technological Utopianism in American Culture* (Chicago: University of Chicago Press, 1985).

2 Ebenezer Howard, "The Transit Problem and the Working Man," *The Town Planning Review*, vol. 4, no. 2 (July 1913), p. 132.

3 K. C. Parsons, "Clarence Stein and the Greenbelt Towns Settling for Less," *Journal of the American Planning Association*, vol. 56, no. 2 (1990), pp. 161–83.

4 "Greenbelt Museum," http://greenbeltmuseum.org/history, accessed July 30, 2015, and Gilbert Cam, "United States Government Activity in Low-Cost Housing, 1932–38," *Journal of Political Economy*, vol. 47, no. 3 (June 1939), pp. 357–78.

5 Walter Agard, "Review of *The Disappearing City*," *The American Magazine of Art*, vol. 25, no. 6 (December 1932), p. 364.

6 Howard Strong, "Regional Planning and Its Relation to the Traffic Problem," *Annals of the American Academy of Political and Social Science*, vol. 133, (September 1927), p. 221.

7 Colin Buchanan, *Traffic in Towns: A Study of the Long Term Problems of Traffic in Urban Areas* (London: Her Majesty's Stationery Office, 1963), p. 42.

8 Buchanan, *Traffic in Towns*, pp. 101–02.

9 N. K. Vaswani, *State of the Art in Management of Traffic in Residential Subdivisions*, VHTRC 77-R48 (Charlottesville: Virginia Highway and Transportation Research Council, 1977).

10 Donald Appleyard, *Livable Streets* (Berkeley: University of California Press, 1981).

11 Project for Public Spaces, "Donald Appleyard," http://www.pps.org/reference/dappleyard/, accessed July 26, 2015.

12 Carmen Hass-Klau, *The Pedestrian and City Traffic* (London: Belhaven Press, 1990).

13 Carmen Hass-Klau et al., *Civilized Streets: A Guide to Traffic Calming* (Brighton: Environmental and Transport Planning, 1992).

Chapter 4

1 Lewis Mumford, *From the Ground Up* (New York: Harcourt, Brace & World, Inc., 1956).

2 Mumford, "The Intolerable City: Must It Keep on Growing?" *Harper's*, February 1926, Sections I-IV, pp. 5–6.

3 Mumford, *The City in History: Its Origins, Its Transformations, and Its Prospects* (New York: Harcourt, Brace and World, Inc., 1961), pp. 486, 509–12.

4 For a discussion of these ideas in depth, see Mumford, *Technics and Civilization* (1934).

5 On the power and influence of Moses, see Robert Caro, *The Power Broker* (New York: Knopf, 1974), which won a Pulitzer Prize. Many people disagreed with Caro's negative characterization of Moses. Moses himself who responded with a twenty-three-page criticism that the biography was "full of mistakes, unsupported charges, nasty, baseless personalities and random haymakers" See Robert Moses, "Comment a New Yorker Profile and Biography," August 26, 1974, at "Robert Moses" Response to Robert Caro's *The Power Broker*, http://www.bridgeandtunnelclub.com/detritus/moses/response.htm, accessed August 4, 2015.

6 Martha Bianco, "Robert Moses and Lewis Mumford: Competing Paradigms of Growth in Portland, Oregon," *Planning Perspectives*, vol. 16 (2001), p. 114.

Chapter 5

1 See for example, Enrique Peñalosa, "Transport as Justice," PPT presentation at Urban Age Johannesburg, South Africa, conference, http://www.casoi.com.br/hjr/pdfs/Enrique_Penalosa.pdf, June 2006.

2 "The World's Biggest Road Networks," January 13, 2014, http://www.roadtraffic-technology.com/features/featurethe-worlds-biggest-road-networks-4159235/.

3 "Bicycle Touring on Car Free Paths," http://bicycletouringoncarfreepaths.org/www Bicycletouringoncarfreepaths.org/Welcome.html, accessed August 19, 2015 and Jeff Baron, Email to the author, August 19, 2015.

4 Ralph Buehler and John Pucher, "Walking and Cycling in Western Europe and the United States," *TR News*, no. 280 (May-June 2012), p. 38.

5 The following paragraphs on road construction are drawn from "The Trailblazers. Brief History of the Direct Federal Highway Construction Program," Federal Highway Administration, US Department of Transportation, October 16, 2013, http://www.fhwa.dot.gov/infrastructure/blazer01.cfm.

6 Ashley Halsey, "Washington Rated the Worst For Traffic—Again," *Washington Post*, February 5, 2013, http://www.washingtonpost.com/local/trafficandcommuting/washington-rated-the-worst-for-traffic-congestion--again/2013/02/04/125be724-6ee3-11e2-8b8d-e0b59a1b8e2a_story.html.

7 P. D. Norton, "Street Rivals: Jaywalking and the Invention of the Motor Age," *Technology and Culture*, vol. 48, no. 2 (April 2007), pp. 331–59.

8 Pyke Johnson, "Herbert Fairbank: Tribute to an Unknown American," *Federal Highway Works Administration*, June 24, 1964, http://www.fhwa.dot.gov/highwayhistory/fairbank.pdf.

9 Richard Weingroff, "Part 2 the Battle of Its Life," *Federal Highway Administration, The Greatest Decade 1956-1966*, October 24, 2013, http://www.fhwa.dot.gov/infrastructure/50interstate2.cfm. See also City of Portland, Oregon, "Speed Bumps," *Portland Bureau of Transportation*, https://www.portlandoregon.gov/transportation/article/83338, accessed August 5, 2015.

10 Rodney van der Ree, Danile J. Smith, and Clara Grillo, *Handbook of Road Ecology* (Hoboken, NJ: John Wiley and Sons, 2015), p. 452.

Chapter 6

1 Thomas Hughes, "The Evolution of Large Technological Systems," in *The Social Construction of Technological Systems,* ed. Wiebe Bijker, Thomas Hughes, and Trevor Pinch, (Cambridge and London: MIT Press, 2012), pp. 45–76. See also Hughes *Rescuing Prometheus* (New York: Pantheon, 1998).

2 J. B. Boer and D. Vermeulen, "Motorcar Headlights," *Philips Technical Review*, vol. 12, no. 11 (1951), pp. 305–17.

3 C. A. Carlquist, "Safe or Dangerous? An International Comparison of Traffic Accident Figures," *Traffic Engineering*, August 1966, pp. 31–5.

4 L. T. B. van Kampen and A. Edelman, *Legislation and Research in the Netherlands in the Field of Traffic Safety Regarding Seat Belts and Crash Helmets*, Publication R-1979-52 (Voorburg: SMOV, 1979).

5 IIHS, "About the Institute," http://www.iihs.org/iihs/about-us, accessed September 17, 2015.

6 The National Academies of Science, Engineering and Medicine, "The Transportation Research Board," http://www.trb.org/AboutTRB/AboutTRB.aspx, accessed September 17, 2015.

7 Bureau of Public Roads, *United States System of Highways Adopted for Uniform Marking by the American Association of State Highway Officials* (Washington: Bureau of Public Roads November 11, 1926).

8 AASHTO, *AASHTO Publications*, vol. 5 (Washington, DC: AASHTO, 2015).

9 Institute of Transportation Engineers, "About ITE," http://www.ite.org/aboutite/index.asp, accessed September 17, 2015.

10 Email communication, Dr. Martin Savelsbergh, to the author, September 17, 2015. Other journals of the field include *Transportation Research Record, Journal of Transport Engineering* (in 2015 at 140 volumes), the more recent *International Journal of Traffic, Transportation Engineering*, and *Modern Traffic and Transportation Engineering Research*.

11 Ed Cline and Jerry Dabkowski, "Traffic Calming—Beware of the Backlash," presented at the ITE International Conference in Kissimmee, FL, March 1999.

12 J. H. Kraay, M. Slop, and S. Oppe, "Safety of Pedestrian Crossings," Publication 1974-2E (Voorburg: SMOV, 1974).

13 J. H. Kraay, "Pedestrian Road Safety Development and Research in the Netherlands," Publication R-1977-16 (Voorsburg: SMOV, 1974). Kray noted that data were incomplete at best and this limited exact conclusions.

14 S. J. Ashton and G. M. Mackay, "Some Characteristics of the Population Who Suffer Trauma as Pedestrians When Hit by Cars and Resulting Implications," Accident Research Unit, University of Birmingham, England, 1979, p. 43, http://webarchive.nationalarchives.gov.uk/+/http:/www.dft.gov.uk/foi/responses/2005/nov/203040message/paperaboutthedepartments20302445.

15 A. A. Vis, A. Dijkstra, and M. Slop, "Safety effects of 30 km/h zones in the Netherlands," *Accidents Analysis and Prevention*, vol. 24, no. 1 (1992), pp. 75–86.

16 Vis, Dijkstra, Slop, "Safety effects," and Vis and I. Kaal, "*De veiligheid van 30 km/luur gebieden*" *(The safety of '3~/cm/h zones'J, R-93-17)* (Leidschendam: SMOV, 1994).

Chapter 7

1 National Automobile Chamber of Commerce, Inc., *Facts and Figures of the Automobile Industry* (New York: National Automobile Chamber of Commerce, Inc., 1921, p. 10.

2 James A. Tobey, "The Hazard of the Automobile," *The Scientific Monthly*, vol. 32, no. 6 (June 1931), pp. 519–21.

3 S. H. Nerlove and W. J. Graham, "The Trend of Personal Automobile Accidents," *The Journal of Business of the University of Chicago*, vol. 1, no. 2 (April 1928), pp. 174–201.

4   Claire Straith, "Management of Facial Injuries Caused by
    Motor Accidents," *JAMA*, vol. 108, no 2 (1937), pp. 101–05,
    and "Guest Passenger Injuries," *JAMA* vol. 137, no. 4 (1948):
    pp. 348–51.

5   http://amhistory.si.edu/onthemove/themes/story_86_10.html.

6   In *Merchants of Doubt* (New York: Bloomsbury, 2010), Erik
    Conway and Naomi Oreskes discuss scientific obfuscation of
    facts by the tobacco, petrochemical, and other industries.

7   Jonathan Philpott et al., "Rectal Blowout by Personal
    Watercraft Water Jet: Case Report and Review of Literature,"
    Journal of Trauma, vol. 47, no. 2 (August 1999), pp. 385–88.
    On the environmental and public health costs of recreational
    machines, see Paul Josephson, *Motorized Obsession*
    (Baltimore: Johns Hopkins University Press, 2007).

Chapter 8

1   John F. Kennedy, "Special Message to the Congress on
    Transportation," *The American Presidency Project,* April
    5, 1962, http://www.presidency.ucsb.edu/ws/?pid=8587.
    See also Richard Weingroff, "Part 2 the Battle of Its Life,"
    *Federal Highway Administration, The Greatest Decade
    1956–1966*, October 24, 2013, http://www.fhwa.dot.gov/
    infrastructure/50interstate2.cfm.

2   S. Harper, T. J. Charters, and E. C. Strumpf, "Trends in
    Socioeconomic Inequalities in Motor Vehicle Accident
    Deaths in the United States, 1995–2010," *American Journal of
    Epidemiology*, vol. 183, no. 7 (October 2015), pp. 606–14.

3 Weingroff, "Part 2 the Battle of Its Life."

4 Warren v. Waterville Urban Renewal Authority, 210 A.2d
   41 (1965). May 12, 1965, http://law.justia.com/cases/maine/
   supreme-court/1965/210-a-2d-41-0.html.

Chapter 9

1 J. Zacharias, "Pedestrian Behavior and Perception in Urban
   Walking Environments," *Journal of Planning Literature*, vol. 16,
   no. 1 (2001), pp. 3–18.

2 Kerstin Hilt, "The Demise of Germany's Pedestrian Zones,"
   June 28, 2005, http://www.dw.com/en/the-demise-of-
   germanys-pedestrian-zones/a-1631633.

3 "Lijnbaan," https://en.rotterdam.info/visitors/places-to-go/
   detail/?id=5092&prefix=shopping&name=lijnbaan, accessed
   August 10, 2015.

4 "Lijnbaan," http://www.architectuurinrotterdam.nl/building.
   php?buildingid=219&lang=en&PHPSESSID=228f4fae13d725
   0ef550110c6208b879, accessed August 10, 2015.

5 "The Pedestrian Street—'Strøget,'" http://www.copenhagenet.
   dk/cph-map/CPH-Pedestrian.asp, accessed October 18, 2015.

6 Jessica Schmidt, "Revisiting Pedestrian Malls," Unpublished
   Paper, http://nacto.org/docs/usdg/revisiting_pedestrian_
   malls_scmidt.pdf., accessed October 18, 2015.

7 Jan Gehl, Jeff Risom, and Julia Day, "Times Square: The Naked
   Truth," *New York Times*, August 31, 2015, http://www.nytimes.
   com/2015/08/31/opinion/times-square-the-naked-truth.
   html?ref=opinion.

Chapter 10

1   S. T. Janssen, "Road Safety in Urban Districts: Final Results of Accident Studies in the Dutch Demonstration Projects of the 1970s," *Traffic Engineering + Control*, vol. 32 (1991), pp. 292–96. On US efforts for neighborhood thinking and its limited success, see Reid Ewing et al., *Traffic Calming: State of the Practice* (Washington, DC: Institute of Transportation Engineers, 1999), pp. 13–14.

2   J. H. Kraay, "Woonerfs and Other Experiments in the Netherlands," *Built Environment*, vol. 12, nos.1/2, (1986), read as Research Paper R-86-23 (Leidschendam, SMOV, 1986), p. 2.

3   Kraay, "Woonerfs," p. 3.

4   Ibid., p. 10.

5   J. H. Kraay, M. P. M. Mathijssen, and F. C. M. Wegman, "De verkeersonveiligheid in woonwijken; Een overzicht van de problemen en mogelijke oplossingen," Research Paper P-1982-1N (SWOV, Leidschendam, 1982), p. 39.

6   Kraay, "Woonerfs," p. 10.

7   Kraay and M. G. Bakker, "Experimenten in verblijfsgebie- den; Verslag van onderzoek naar de effecten van infrastructurele maatregelen op verkeersongevallen," Research Paper R-84-50 (SWOV, Leidschendam, 1984) and Kraay, "Traffic safety in reconstructed streets," Lecture presented at the Technical University, Espoo, Finland, May 14, 1985. Paper R-85-39 (Sway, Leidschendam, 1985).

Chapter 11

1 A. G. Welleman, "Water Nuisance and Road Safety," SMOV paper R-78-5 (Voorburg: Institute for Road Safety Research, 1978).

2 Frederick S. Benson, "Highway Safety: The Death Penalty Has Not Been Abolished," *The Forum (Section of Insurance, Negligence and Compensation Law, American Bar Association)*, vol. 4, no. 4 (July 1969), pp. 308–12.

3 "DOT Lacks Vigorous Hazard Removal Program," *Insurance Institute for Highway Safety Status Report*, October 16, 1972, vol. 7, no. 19, October 16, 1972, p. 1.

4 Bruce Lambert, "John A. Blatnik, 80, Congressman Who Promoted Public Works Bills," New York Times, December 19, 1991, http://www.nytimes.com/1991/12/19/us/john-a-blatnik-80-congressman-who-promoted-public-works-bills.html.

5 John Blatnik, "The Need for Highway Safety Consciousness," in John Blatnik and Charles W. Prisk, *Roadside Hazards* (Saugatuck, CT: Eno Foundation for Highway Traffic Control, Inc., 1968), pp. 1–2.

6 Blatnik, "The Need for Highway," pp. 3–5.

7 On the early median philosophy, see F. C. Flury, "Lecture on Median Barriers," SMOV (Voorburg, SMOV, 1966).

8 Ibid.

9 Transportation Research Board, National Research Council, "Guardrail and Median Barrier Crashworthiness," NCHRP Synthesis 244 Washington, DC: NRC, 1997).

10 Scott Kozel, "New Jersey Median Barrier History," November 22, 1997, www.roadstothefuture.com/Jersey_barrier.html.

11 Charles F. McDevitt, "Basics of Concrete Barriers," *Public Roads*, vol. 63, no. 5 (March/April 2000), http://fhwicsint01.fhwa.dot.gov/publications/publicroads/00marapr/concrete.cfm, accessed June 29, 2015.

12 Zoe Szathmary, "Golden Gate Bridge Reopens After $30 Million Safety Barrier is Installed to Protect against Head-on Collisions," January 12, 2015, http://www.dailymail.co.uk/news/article-2906386/Traffic-flows-Golden-Gate-Bridge-safety-barrier-added.html#ixzz3eRZzx14e.

13 "Unlighted Signs Glow in Automotive Headlights," *Science News*, vol. 62 (July 12, 1952), p. 24.

14 SMOV, "Hazards with Falling Lighting Columns: Considerations Regarding the Positioning of Lighting Columns Low-Aggressive for Private Car," SMOV report 1978-3E (Voorburg: SWOV, 1978); D. A. Schreuder, "Safety Barriers and Lighting Columns," *International Lighting Review*, vol. 23 (1972), pp. 20–2; and Dan W. Hoyt, "In Further Support of Rumble Strips," *Traffic Engineering*, November 1968, pp. 38–41.

15 Ian Wylie, "'Traffic Lights are So Dictatorial' . . . but are Roundabouts on the Way Out?" October 19, 2015, http://www.theguardian.com/cities/2015/oct/19/traffic-lights-roundabouts-way-out.

16 J. van Minnen, "Experiences with New Roundabouts in The Netherlands," D-92-0 (Leidschendam: SMOV, 1992); Royal Kaskoning DHV, *Roundabouts—Application and Design: A Practical Manual* (Amersfoort, Netherlands: Ministry of Transport, Public Works and Water Management: June 2009), pp. 27–31; and Lee August Rodegerdts, *Roundabouts:*

An Informational Guide (Washington, DC: Transportation Research Board, 2010), p. 5–20.

17 J. van Minnen, *Ongevallen op rotondes*, R-90-47 (Leidschendam: SMOV, 1990).

18 Municipality of Carmel, Indiana, *Benefits of Roundabouts*, brochure, pdf, 2008(?).

Chapter 12

1 Julie Peterson, "Smashing Barriers to Access: Disability Activism and Curb Cuts," July 15, 2015, http://americanhistory.si.edu/blog/smashing-barriers-access-disability-activism-and-curb-cuts.

2 Sarah Phillips, "'There Are No Invalids in the USSR!': A Missing Soviet Chapter in the New Disability History," *Disability Studies Quarterly*, vol. 29, no. 3 (2009), http://dsq-sds.org/article/view/936/1111.

3 Bess Williamson, "The People's Sidewalks," *Boom*, vol. 2, no. 1 (Spring 2012), http://www.boomcalifornia.com/2012/06/the-peoples-sidewalks/.

4 Carole E. Hill and Mary Lou Grabbe, "GSU: Wheelchairs Are Welcome," *Change*, vol. 9, no. 3 (March 1977), pp. 19–21.

5 Eric R. Breslin, "Backlash Against the Disabled," *Mental Disability Law Reporter*, vol. 4, no. 5 (September-October 1980), p. 355.

6 See "Barden v. Sacramento: Landmark Case Establishes Nationwide Standard for Public Sidewalks," http://www.dralegal.org/impact/cases/barden-v-sacramento, accessed August 16, 2015. See the legal opinion http://www.dralegal.org/sites/dralegal.org/files/casefiles/uscaopinion.pdf. The US

Supreme Court refused to hear an appeal on the case that let stand the ruling of the 9th Circuit Court.

7 Jennifer Steinhauer, "Dole Appears, but G.O.P. Rejects a Disability Treaty," *New York Times*, December 4, 2012, http://www.nytimes.com/2012/12/05/us/despite-doles-wish-gop-rejects-disabilities-treaty.html.

8 "Concerns About Manhattan Curb Cuts Designed to Help Disabled," July 28, 2015, http://www.nbcnewyork.com/news/local/Manhattan-Curb-Cuts-NYC-Sidewalks-Disabled-People-Access-Obstructed-Nonexistent-319033621.html.

Chapter 13

1 US Census Bureau, Census 1960, 1970, 1980, 1990, and American Community Survey 2013; Steven Ruggles et al., *Integrated Public Use Microdata Series: Version 5.0.* Minneapolis: University of Minnesota. 2010.

2 Ibid.

3 "Dutch Commutes are the Longest in Europe," *View from the Cycle Path*, December 6, 2011 http://www.aviewfromthecyclepath.com/2011/12/are-your-travel-distances-and-times-too.html.

4 Buehler and Pucher, "Walking and Cycling."

5 F. C. M. Wegman, "Urban Planning, Traffic Planning and Traffic Safety of Pedestrians and Cyclists," SMOV 79-7 (Voorburg, Institute for Road Safety Research, 1979).

6 Buehler and Pucher, "Walking and Cycling." p. 38.

7 Ibid., p. 39.

8 Ibid., p. 41.

Chapter 14

1 A. I. King et al., "Humanitarian Benefits of Cadaver Research on Injury Prevention," *Journal of Trauma*, vol. 38, no. 4 (April 1995), pp. 564–69.

2 Merritt Roe Smith, "Introduction," in Merritt Roe Smith, *Military Enterprise and Technological Change,* (Cambridge: MIT Press, 1985), pp. 1–38.

3 Gilian Holmes, "Crash Test Dummy," *How Things Are Made*, http://www.madehow.com/Volume-5/Crash-Test-Dummy.html#ixzz3fD2v5KqI accessed July 7, 2015.

4 "Deliberate Crashes May Save Many Lives," *The Science News-Letter*, vol. 71, no. 5 (February 2, 1957), p. 78.

5 Edward Housman, "Crash-Proofing Drivers," *The Science News-Letter*, vol. 68, no. 16 (October 15, 1955), pp. 250–52.

6 "Crash Test Dummies," http://www.iihs.org/iihs/about-us/vrc, accessed June 21, 2015.

7 "Pregnant Crash Test Dummies: Rethinking Standards and Reference Models," Gendered Innovations In Science, Health and Medicine, Engineering, and Environment, https://genderedinnovations.stanford.edu/case-studies/crash.html#tabs-2, accessed June 21, 2015.

8 See for example C. D. Matthews, "Incorrectly Used Seat Belt Associated with Uterine Rupture Following Vehicular Collision," *American Journal of Obstetrics and Gynecology*, vol. 121, no. 8 (April 15,1975), pp. 1115–16.

9 "Pregnant Crash Test Dummies." On effects of crashes on fetal outcomes, see Catherine Vladutiu and Harold Weiss, "Motor Vehicle Safety during Pregnancy," *American Journal of Lifestyle Medicine*, vol. 6, no. 3 (2012), pp. 241–49.

Chapter 15

1 Jameson Wetmore, "Delegating to the Automobile: Experimenting with Automotive Restraints in the 1970s," *Technology and Culture*, vol. 56, no. 2 (April 2015), p. 441.

2 "Chronology of Events Involving Air Bags," July 12, 1984, *New York Times*, http://www.nytimes.com/1984/07/12/us/chronology-of-events-involving-air-bags.html.

3 Research on lighting far preceded use of research for safety standards. See C. H. Sharp et al., "Automobile Headlighting Regulation," *Scientific American Monthly*, vol. 1 (April 1920), p. 347–50. As noted in a 1923 article, "If all Headlights could be Focused in the Same Manner, this would Simplify the Instructions Required and Facilitate Adjustment." See "The Adjustment of Headlights," *Science*, vol. 58, no. 1504 (October 26, 1923) p. 327.

4 "Why Auto Safety Legislation Was Necessary," *Consumer Bulletin*, vol. 50 (June 1967), p. 33–35.

5 Wetmore, "Delegating," p. 440.

6 For the same arguments about individual freedom versus paternalism and motorcycle fatalities that have risen significantly since the repeal of helmet laws, see Insurance Institute for Highway Safety, "Motorcycle, Truck Safety Highlighted in Revised Five Year Plan," *High Loss Reduction Status Report*, vol. 14, no. 7 (April 1979), pp. 3–4; Stacy Dickert-Conlin, Todd Elder and Brian Moore, "Donorcycles: Motorcycle Helmet Laws and the Supply of Organ Donors," Michigan State University, November 18, 2010, unpublished paper on line; and Marian Jones and Ronald Bayer, "Paternalism & Its Discontents: Motorcycle Helmet Laws, Libertarian Values, and Public Health," *American Journal of Public Health*, vol. 97, no. 2 (February 2007), pp. 208–17.

7 "Road Accidents: Seat Belts and the Safe Car," *The British Medical Journal*, vol. 2, no. 6153 (December 16, 1978), pp. 1695–98.

8 Wetmore, "Delegating," p. 442.

Chapter 16

1 John D. Graham and Patricia Gorham, "NHTSA and Passive Restraints: A Case of Arbitrary and Capricious Deregulation," *Administrative Law Review*, vol. 35, no. 2 (Spring 1983), pp. 193–95.

2 Philip Heyman, *The Politics of Public Management* (New Haven: Yale University Press, 1987), pp. 85–88.

3 Graham and Gorham, pp. 245–47. On this topic Jamison Wetmore points out that "Federal rules, however, prohibited the NHSB from mandating a specific technology. Instead the NHSB had to shape its regulations around 'design criteria.'" See Wetmore, "Delegating," pp. 443–44.

4 NHTSA Regulations, http://www.nhtsa.gov/cars/problems/studies/Bumper/Index.html.

5 Congressman Louis Wyman, "The Case Against Seat-Belt Interlocks," *Motor Trend*, vol. 26 (May 1974): p. 53–.

Chapter 17

1 Novosti Belarusi, "'Spiashchie Politseiskie'" Uvelichivaiut Vrednye Vybrosy v 12 Raz," September 11, 2104, http://www.abw.by/news/177516/.

2 Kyoungho Ahn and Hesham Rakha, "Energy and Environmental Effects of Traffic Calming Measures," Paper Presented at the 87th Annual Meeting of the TRB, Washington, DC, 2008.

3 van Schagen, *Traffic Calming Schemes*, pp. 11–12.

4 T. F. Fwa and C. Y. Liaw, "Rational Approach for Geometric Design of Speed-Control Road Hump," in *Operational Effects of Geometrics and Geometric Design* (Washington, DC: Transportation Research Board, 1992), pp. 66–72.

Chapter 18

1 Luisa Zottis, "As Europe's Traffic Fatalities Drop, Brazil's Soar," *The City Fix*, April 8, 2014, http://thecityfix.com/blog/europes-traffic-fatalities-drop-brazils-soar-luisa-zottis/.

2 Eduardo Vasconcellos, Michael Sivak, "Road Safety in Brazil: Challenges and Opportunities," Report UMTRI-2009-29 (Ann Arbor, Michigan: University of Michigan Transportation Research Institute, August 2009).

3 A. Chandran et al., "Road Traffic Deaths in Brazil: Rising Trends in Pedestrian and Motorcycle Occupant Deaths," *Traffic Injury Prevention*, vol. 13, supplement 1 (2012): pp. 11–16.

4 Ministério das Cidades, Comitê Nacional de Mobilização Pela Saúde, Segurança e Paz no Trânsito, *Plano Nacional de Redução de Acidentes e Segurança Viária Para a Década 2011–2020* (Brasilia: Ministério das Cidades, December 8, 2010), http://www.denatran.gov.br/download/Plano%20Nacional%20 de%20Redu%C3%A7%C3%A3o%20de%20Acidentes%20 -%20Comite%20-%20Proposta%20Preliminar.pdf.

5 World Health Organization, "Road Safety in Brazil," from *Global Status Report on Road Safety 2013*, http://www.who.int/violence_injury_prevention/road_traffic/countrywork/bra/en/, accessed July 6, 2015.

6 Editorial Board, "A Foolish Attempt to Weaken Truck Safety," *New York Times*, May 26, 2015, http://www.nytimes.com/2015/05/26/opinion/a-foolish-attempt-to-weaken-truck-safety.html.

7 Howard Abramson, "The Trucks Are Killing Us," August 21, 2015, *New York Times*, http://www.nytimes.com/2015/08/22/opinion/the-trucks-are-killing-us.html?ref=opinion&_r=0.

8 World Health Organization, "Road Safety in Brazil," accessed August 12, 2015, http://www.who.int/violence_injury_prevention/road_traffic/countrywork/bra/en/.

9 Alan Clendenning, "Paving of Road Brings Change in the Amazon Rainforest," May 28, 2005, http://news.mongabay.com/2005/0527-ap.html#y1dWZ9f1WXJS6276.99.

10 "Famosa rua de São Joaquim ganha duas lombadas para redução de velocidade," June 25, 2014, http://saojoaquimonline.com.br/2014/06/25/famosa-rua-de-sao-joaquim-ganha-duas-lombadas-para-reducao-de-velocidade/.

11 "No Sertão Populares interdita BR 230 reivindicando lombadas," June 22, 2015, http://uirauna.net/no-sertao-populares-interdita-br-230-reivindicando-lombadas/.

12 Gringo Guru, "Bumps," in *Gringo's Guide*, http://www.drivemeloco.com/mexico-speed-bumps/, accessed October 24, 2015.

13 Chris Zelkovich, "The Confusing Signs and Scary Speed Bumps of Mexico's Yucatan," *The Globe and Mail*, July 3, 2015, http://www.theglobeandmail.com/globe-drive/culture/

commentary/driving-the-yucatan-is-a-magical-mystery-tour-filled-with-strange-traffic-signs/article25227027/, accessed October 24, 2015.

14 "DNIT conclui instalação de três lombadas eletrônicas no contorno da BR 230 em Cajazeiras," June 20, 2014, http://portalczn.com.br/dnit-conclui-instalacao-de-tres-lombadas-eletronicas-no-contorno-da-br-230-em-cajazeiras/.

15 See www.detran.rn.gov.br/Equipamentos Eletrô Governo do Estado do Rio Grande do Norte—Departamento Estadual de Transito do Rio Grande do Norte—Detran and http://www.perkons.com/pt/produtos-e-sistemas-detalhes/14/lombada-eletronica#sthash.7lT1toHa.dpuf.

16 "Novos radares e lombadas funcionarão a partir desta sexta," June 20, 2012, http://www.pbagora.com.br/conteudo.php?id=2 0120620171039&cat=paraiba&keys=novos-radares-lombadas-funcionarao-partir-desta-sexta.

Chapter 19

1 "You are my last love, My car, my car. You and I got drunk again, My one and only. The taste of gasoline is like coffee. Day and night I am breathing time, and we're living together. We will have a car, you are my sun."

2 Stan Lugar, *Corporate Power, American Democracy, and the Automobile Industry* (New York: Cambridge University Press, 2000).

3 Lewis Siegelbaum, *Cars for Comrades* (Ithaca: Cornell University Press, 2008)

4 Jeff Bennett and John Stoll, "GM to Close Russian Assembly Plant," *Wall Street Journal*, March 18, 2015, http://www.

wsj.com/articles/gm-to-indefinitely-idle-russian-assembly-plant-1426681831.

5   Olga Kazan, "A Surprising Map of Countries that Have the Most Traffic Deaths," January 18, 2013, *Washington Post*, https://www.washingtonpost.com/blogs/worldviews/wp/2013/01/18/a-surprising-map-of-countries-that-have-the-most-traffic-deaths/.

6   "Latest Russian Accident Statistic Published," August 19, 2014, http://rsrussia.org/events/read/latest_russian_accident_statistics_published-274/

7   Jeanne Breen et al., *Road Safety Performance. National Peer Review: Russian Federation* (OECD International Transport Forum, 2011), p. 3.

8   NHTSA, "Seat Belt Use in 2013—Use Rates in the States and Territories," DOT HS 812 030, May 2014 (US DOT: NHTSA, 2014).

9   S. Ma, et al., "Seat Belt and Child Seat Use in Lipetskaya Oblast, Russia: Frequencies, Attitudes, and Perceptions," *Traffic Injury Prevention*, vol. 13 (2012), Supplement 1: pp. 76–81, and "Kazhdaia Trinadtsataia Avariia v Rossii Proiskhodit po Vine P'ianykh Voditelei," September 8, 2013, https://news.mail.ru/incident/15095962/. See also "Latest Russian Accident Statistics Published," August 19, 2014, *Road Safety Russia* http://rsrussia.org/events/read/latest_russian_accident_statistics_published-274/.

10   "Korruptsiia v Dorozhnom Stroitel'stve," June 10, 2011, http://zlovesti.ru/korruptsiya-v-dorozhnom-stroitelstve.html.

11   "Korruptsiia."

12   Anton Chablin, "Dorogi, Vedushchie v Ad. Korruptsiia v Dorozhnom Storitel'stve na Stavropol'e," June 24, 2015, http://

onkavkaz.com/articles/363-dorogi-veduschie-v-ad-korrupcija-
v-dorozhnom-stroitelstve-na-stavropole.html.

13 Dmitrii Zhuravlev, "Tri Kita Dorozhnoi Korruptsii," March 28,
    2015, http://www.aif.ru/auto/opinion/1474410.

14 "Most Cherez Kerchenskii Proliv v Krym Otrkoiut k Kontsu
    2018 goda," January 30, 2015, http://www.5-tv.ru/news/93748/.

15 Anti-Corruption Foundation, *Sochi 2014: Comprehensive
    Report*, http://sochi.fbk.info/en/

16 "Postavka Materialov dlia Mosta v Obkhod Naselennykh
    Punktov," July 11, 2015, http://most-kerch.org/.

17 "Dorozhnye Iamy v Samare Izmeriali v Prisutstvii Sotrudnikov
    Prokuratury," May 26, 2015, http://www.tvsamara.ru/news/11138/.

18 See http://www.dorogibezproblem.ru/and "Dorozhnye Iamy."

19 "V Apatitakh na Dorozhnye Iamy Nanosiat Razmetku," June
    15, 2015, http://www.hibiny.com/news/archive/80190.

20 "Dorozhnye Iamy v Petropavlovske-Kamchatskom Zadelali
    Faneroi," April 29, 2015, http://www.tvc.ru/news/show/
    id/67254.

21 "V Primor'e Voditeli Zasipali Iamu na Doroge Den'gami,
    Zaiaviv, chto Dorozhnye Nalogi ne Rabotaiut," March
    31, 2015, at http://auto.newsru.ru/article/31mar2015/
    dorogimoney.

22 "Lezhachii Politseiskii," http://www.vashamashina.ru/lpolice.
    html, accessed July 11, 2015.

23 Timofei Borisov, "Prover' Lezhachego," *Rossiiskaia Gazeta*, July
    26, 2011, http://www.rg.ru/2011/07/26/police.html.

24 "Lezhachie Politseiskie," *Avtolikbez*, March 22, 2010, http://
    www.avtolikbez.ru/?an=thread&thread=502768222.

25 "V Ekaterinburge 'Lezhachie Politseiskie,'" *Regiony Online*, August 17, 2014, at http://www.gosrf.ru/news/15721/.

26 "Foto Ochevidtsa: V Syktyvkare Poiavilsia Eshche Odin 'Lezhachii Politseiskii,'" *ProGorodSyktyvkar,* June 20, 2015, http://progorod11.ru/auto/view/185613.

27 "V Omske Poiavitsia Eshche 37 'Lezhachikh Politseiskikh,'" *Argumenty i Fakty*, June 9, 2015, http://www.omsk.aif.ru/zkh/zkh_gorod/v_omske_poyavitsya_eshchyo_37_lezhachih_policeyskih.

28 "Vologzhanam Predstoit Reshit', 'Gde Razmestit' 'Lezhachikh Politseiskikh,'" *Russkaia Planeta*, August 7, 2015, http://vologda.rusplt.ru/index/vologjanam-predstoit-reshit-gde-razmestit-lejachih-politseyskih-407957.html.

29 "Na Ulitsakh Permi Poiavitsia 55 'Lezhachikh Politseiskikh,'" *Novosti@Mail.ru*, August 5, 2015, https://news.mail.ru/inregions/volgaregion/59/society/22887846/.

30 "V Irkutske Poiaviatsia 7 Novykh Sevtoforov, 'Lezhachie Politseiskie' i Dorozhnye Ograzhdeniia Obshchei Protiazhennost'iu 8 Tysiach Pogonnykh Metrov,"*SIA*, May 27, 2015, http://sia.ru/?section=484&action=show_news&id=303510.

31 Lord Velder, "Zhiteli Tveri ne Mogut Dobit'sia Ustanovki Lezhachikh Politseiskikh na Avariinom Uchastke Dorogi," *Tverigrad.ru*, September 6, 2015, http://tverigrad.ru/tblog/zhiteli-tveri-ne-mogut-dobitsya-ustanovki-lezhachikh-policejjskikh-na-avarijjnom-uchastke-dorogi.

32 Peter Spinella, "Moscow and St. Petersburg Lead Europe in Traffic Jams," *The Moscow Times*, April 1, 2015, http://www.themoscowtimes.com/news/article/moscow-and-st-petersburg-lead-europe-in-traffic-jams/518394.html.

33 Svetlana Basharova, "Peshekhody Prevratiat v 'Lezhachikh Politseiskikh'," *Izvestiia*, March 27, 2013, http://izvestia.ru/news/547451#ixzz3j4nRjcS4.

Chapter 20

1 Mike Esbester and Jameson Wetmore, "Global Perspectives on Road Safety History," *Technology and Culture*, vol. 56, no 2, April 2015, pp. 307–18.

2 Thomas Dietz et al., "Political Influences on Greenhouse Gas Emissions in US Sates," *PNAS Early Edition*, pp. 1–8, May 2015.

3 Reid Ewing et al., "Relationship Between Urban Sprawl and Physical Activity, Obesity, and Morbidity," *The Science of Health Promotion*, vol. 18, no. 1 (September/October 2003), p. 57.

INDEX

Note: Page references for illustrations appear in *italics*.

ACKNOWLEDGMENT

I thank Willie "Pops" Stargell and Roberto Clemente for their inspiration in all things leading to this book.